healing
the five
wounds
of the
heart

D1078771

healing the five wounds of the heart

Free Yourself from the Bonds of the Past

DR. MARIE MBOUNI

Hierophantpublishing

Cover design by Adrian Morgan
Cover art by Shutterstock
Print book interior design by Frame25 Productions

Hierophant Publishing
San Antonio, TX
www.hierophantpublishing.com

If you are unable to order this book from your local bookseller, you may order directly from the publisher.

Library of Congress Control Number: 2023940730
ISBN: 978-1-950253-43-2

10 9 8 7 6 5 4 3 2 1

To my grandmother, who endured significant loss and hardship throughout her life, and yet never lost her resilience or her capacity for love. Your strength and grace have inspired me, and I am grateful for the love and wisdom you shared with me.

And to the child within each of us, who carries within them the wounds of the heart, and yet remains capable of boundless love, joy, and wonder. I honor your courage and resilience and am committed to helping you heal and grow into the fullness of your being.

May this book be a tribute to the healing power of love, and a testament to the strength and beauty of the human spirit.

Contents

Introduction

Have you ever found yourself repeating a pattern you swore you'd never get caught in again? Maybe you're doing too much for everyone around you, wearing a mask to make your neighbors or coworkers like you, putting up with a partner who treats you badly, or sacrificing your own goals to please somebody else. You might find yourself thinking, *Why is this happening again?* Yet no matter how many times you resolve to do things differently, the same situations seem to come into your life over and over, as if they are magnetically drawn to you.

As a shaman and energy healer, I see this kind of thing all the time. People come to me because they seem to be caught in an infinite loop. Although they may know on an intellectual level what their problems are, they don't seem to be able to make the deep changes required to "graduate" from these particular modules in their soul's education. They may speak about past traumas with insight, yet it is clear to me from their voice, body language, and manner of being that these traumas are still driving their lives in powerful ways.

After working with hundreds of clients over the span of more than a decade, I noticed a pattern emerging. The people who came to me were all wounded in one of five core ways: They had been abandoned. They had been betrayed. They had been forced to deny their true selves. They had been judged. Or they had been cut off from a sense of connection with other people and with the divine — in short, they had been separated.

They expressed these wounds in their choices of jobs, partners, and friends; in their choice of clothing, music, and books; in their attention or inattention to grooming and exercise; in the harshness or laxness of their inner critic; and in how they presented themselves to me. Although none of them seemed to realize it, these wounds were like filters determining their entire reality. Often, they didn't seem able to see past the limited options their wounds presented to them. Their wounds had become their worlds.

Abandonment, betrayal, denial, judgment, and separation. These are the five wounds of the heart — the five ways we become locked in perpetual suffering. Although we receive these wounds as children, they continue to play out in our adult lives, causing us to unconsciously seek out endless variations on the original painful experience.

Left untreated, the five wounds of the heart lead to repetition compulsion, also known as trauma reenactment—the mysterious effect by which humans seek out the very same situations that hurt them in the past. A person wounded by judgment will continue to judge themselves, or unconsciously seek out shaming partners. A person wounded by betrayal will keep trusting the wrong people, ignoring all evidence that they should run the other way. A single, formative abandonment turns into a series of abandonments. An experience of aloneness turns into a lifetime of separation.

This is not because our wounds *want* us to suffer, however—in fact, quite the opposite. Repetition compulsion is life's way of giving us opportunities to heal. Although we cannot time travel to the past and change things, we *can* heal the past by responding to our present situation in new ways. In this book, I will give you the tools to do exactly that. By bringing your awareness, imagination, creativity, and courage to these practices, you can heal your heart wounds and step into a life of wholeness, ease, and good health.

Identifying Your Heart Wounds

Our deepest wounds are often hidden from ourselves, although they may be painfully obvious to the people around us. This is because we have grown up with them—they seem normal to us, and hence are invisible. For example, if you grew up with a mother who required you to create a false self to please her, you may believe that creating a false self is just a normal requirement of being loved. If you grew up with a father who required you to endlessly forgive or ignore his painful betrayals, you may accept frequent betrayal as a normal condition of being in relationship with others.

Have you ever had a medical condition you were completely unaware of until somebody else pointed it out to you? For example, maybe you were nearsighted as a child, but you didn't realize that other kids could see the blackboard or make out individual leaves on a tree until your teacher pointed it out. Or maybe you have seasonal affective disorder, but it was years or decades before you realized that not everybody becomes debilitatingly depressed in the winter.

We all take our own experience of the world as "normal," to such an extent that we fail to seek out help for even painful, debilitating problems—instead, we chalk them up to being "just the way things are." But what if I told you that the most painful and confounding problems in your life are *not* "just the way things are"—they are wounds that can be healed, putting an end to those problems for good? As a shaman, I've devoted my life to helping people identify and heal their heart wounds. My hope is that this book will achieve the same effect, even if you and I never meet in person.

Take a look at the following descriptions. Does one of these wounds describe your own situation?

Abandonment: You keep getting involved with people and institutions who leave you high and dry. No matter how much you give to others, you keep finding yourself alone right when you need other people the most. Alternatively, important people in your life complain that *you* abandon *them*, no matter how many times you resolve not to do this.

Betrayal: You keep getting involved with people and institutions who break your trust by lying, cheating, stealing, or spreading rumors about you. No matter how carefully you vet your friends and partners, they still end up betraying you. Alternatively, you have a pattern of betraying the important people in your life, no matter how many times you resolve to treat them well.

Denial: You keep getting involved with people and institutions who require you to bury your true self and put up a false front. No matter how firmly you resolve to be yourself, you end up developing a new persona to please others. Alternatively, important people in your life have told you that they can't be their true selves around you, with the result that your relationships are never as close as you would like.

Judgment: You keep getting involved with people and institutions who criticize and shame you, and your response to life's stressors is to criticize and shame yourself. No matter how hard you try to seek out supportive partners and friends, you end up with people who put you down. Alternatively, important people in your life have told you that your constant criticisms are pushing them away.

Separation: You keep getting involved with people or institutions who make you feel like you're all alone. No matter how hard you try to connect with other people, you still feel cut off and isolated. Alternatively, important people in your life have told you that it's difficult to connect with you or make you part of a group, no matter how hard they try to include you.

In many cases, you will immediately recognize yourself in a certain wound. Just reading those five words, *abandonment, betrayal, denial, judgment,* and *separation,* is often enough to make a light bulb go off. Maybe all or some of those words evoke vivid and specific childhood memories—maybe the mere act of reading them makes your stomach knot up and your palms sweat. In other cases, you may think, *There's no way that one applies to me,* only to discover a glaring wound you didn't realize you had.

Even if you remember very little of your childhood, you can identify the heart wounds that are dominating your life by paying careful attention to your own behavior, especially as it pertains to relationships with other people. Do you avoid people? Do you give too much? Do you build walls against intimacy? Do you constantly feel like an outsider? Do you keep finding yourself in relationships with partners who lie to you, abandon you, shut you out emotionally, or require you to put up a false front?

In each of the sections that make up this book, I provide lists of "symptoms" for each heart wound, as well as examples from my own life and the lives of my clients. By carefully reviewing these physical, emotional, and behavioral symptoms, you can identify how active a certain wound is in your life, whether or not you remember the exact origins of the wound. And by working with the healing practices in every other chapter, you can gently defuse your heart wounds and restore yourself to a state of wholeness and balance.

Most adults have all five wounds to some degree. By the time we're in our twenties, most of us have experienced some form of abandonment, betrayal, denial, judgment, or separation of our authentic selves. With this in mind, I encourage you to work with *all* the healing practices in this book, not just the ones associated with your most prominent or obvious wound. By working with all five wounds, you can heal your whole heart—and unlock the hidden treasures that have been waiting for you all along.

The Abandonment Wound

When I was a baby, my mother divorced my dad. She left me and my sister with our grandmother and went to live in Europe with her new husband. The first time I was conscious of the fact that my grandmother wasn't my mother, I was three years old. My mother had flown to Cameroon to visit us. I remember staring at her in confusion, trying to figure out who this strange woman was. If this woman was my mother, as she claimed, then who was my grandmother? Why did I live with my grandma instead of my mom? Why did my mom live in a country far away, and why had she come back?

When my mom left again after a few days, I was even more confused. Mothers were supposed to stay with their children. Why was my mother leaving me behind? Didn't she want me? The excitement I'd begun to feel about being reunited with my mother swiftly turned to sorrow.

A few years later, when I was seven, my father appeared suddenly to take me and my sister away from our grandmother's house. Apparently, he and my mom had made an agreement that he would come and take us when we were "old enough"—but no one had thought to explain this to us. One day, we were living at our grandmother's place; the next day, we were heading out with a father we barely knew, to go live with a stepmother and stepsiblings we had never met.

This time, I felt abandoned by my grandmother. Why was she letting him take us? Why didn't she fight to keep us, or put up any kind of protest at all? Didn't she love us? Other kids lived in one house, with one caregiver or set of caregivers, until they grew up. Why didn't we deserve as good as them? Although I missed my grandmother like crazy, my grief was complicated by anger and confusion. How could she do this to us, knowing our mother had already done it once before?

This pattern of abandonment continued throughout my childhood. When I was thirteen, my mother came back from Europe and scooped me and my sister up from our father's house—only to deliver us to a boarding school in a strange city. Again and again, we were treated like toys that could be picked up, moved around, and cast aside when the adults lost interest. No matter what I did to win my mother's approval and make her want to be with me, I felt like I could never be "good enough" to hold her attention and make her stay.

Even though this pattern of abandonment seems like an obvious source of trauma, it actually took me a lot of work to realize that my family's behavior had affected me at all. I went to medical school and became a successful anesthesiologist. Because I was successful, I believed I hadn't been wounded. But as an adult, I began to wonder, *What's going on with me? I'm single, I'm alone, I don't trust people.* I was cagey and aloof, and although I could put on a good show at cocktail parties, I had a hard time getting close and being vulnerable. If somebody was nice to me, I'd think, *Wait, what do they want from me?*

I didn't bother putting much effort into my relationships, because I assumed that anyone who claimed to care about me would just disappear. As a result of this assumption about my friends, I ended up abandoning *them*—moving away without saying goodbye, ghosting people, and generally treating other people as if they were disposable and interchangeable. Without realizing it, I had begun to treat others the way I had been treated.

After a few years of painful confusion, I did a self-guided shamanic journey in which I traveled back to my childhood. I found myself at age three, and I saw an image of my mother and her new husband. They were wearing matching outfits, and holding pinkies. The thought that came to me was, *What would it take for my mother to hold my hand like that?*

That was when I began to realize that I was living from an abandonment wound, which was affecting my life in countless ways.

I realized I had made several unspoken agreements with myself, in an effort to protect myself from future abandonment. For example, one of my agreements was, "It's OK not to have love." When I realized this, I was stunned. I had decided that it was fine for me to live my whole life without love—either giving it or receiving it. Imagine deciding that it was OK not to give a baby love, or a puppy or a cat—or even a houseplant! We cannot survive without love. Yet I had decided that this was an acceptable way for me to live.

As soon as I realized that I was starving myself of love, I decided to change my life. I resolved that from that point on, I would always give and receive love. I would no longer let my abandonment wound run my life from the shadows—I would bring it into the light and let it heal. Most importantly, I would never again abandon myself. I would become my own best friend, staying loyal to myself in times of hardship and trouble, and never questioning my own worth.

Origins of the Abandonment Wound

We all feel abandoned from time to time—whether it's by a friend who fails to show up when we need her, by a sibling who declines to help with aging parents, or by a customer service agent who leaves us on hold for hours when we're trying to solve a stressful problem. Humans are deeply social creatures, and abandonment activates our threat response, while flooding us with sensations of deep distress: *Where is the tribe? I need them! I can't do this on my own!*

Although most of us can tolerate the occasional, small instance of abandonment, we can develop an abandonment wound when the stakes are high and the distress is unmitigated for long periods of time. Physical abandonment by a parent is just one of a variety of ways people can develop an abandonment wound. Other causes can include the following:

- Grieving the death of a parent or caregiver
- Being affected by a parent or caregiver's alcoholism or addiction

- Having neglectful parents

- Being left home alone as a child

- Being abandoned by a spouse

- Being left to deal with an overwhelming situation at a young age

- Enduring the intolerable; the sense of being abandoned by God

This last one—being abandoned by God—is especially difficult. A client of mine had a loving husband and family and all the support she could wish for, but when her six-year-old child died of leukemia she experienced a nearly unbearable sense of abandonment. In this sense, abandonment involves the breaking of an unwritten contract—between parents and children, or between God and humanity. We feel abandoned when the person or deity who was supposed to love and protect us withdraws that love and protection, leaving us alone with unmanageable pain.

Signs You Are Living with an Abandonment Wound

A client of mine was constantly giving gifts. She would make cookies for the mail carrier, press food and drinks on anyone who walked through her door, and give away clothes, books, or garden tools to anyone who she thought might like them. Not only that, but she was constantly offering to do things for her neighbors and friends, even when nobody had asked. Although people often started out by gratefully accepting her gifts, it was only a matter of time before new acquaintances began to decline her offers, which caused my client enormous anxiety.

Generosity is a beautiful thing within appropriate limits—but my client's giving had an edge of neediness to it that drove others away. She unconsciously believed that by giving things to people, she could force them to be friends with her, and prevent them from abandoning her. Before we began our work together, she had no idea that this chronic gift-giving had anything to do with the abandonment she had experienced as a child.

The abandonment wound can show itself in surprising ways. You may be living with an abandonment wound if any of these situations ring true for you:

- You have a desperate need to please others.

- You constantly seek reassurance that you are loved and valued.

- You avoid commitment.

- You assume others will leave you.

- You leave romantic partners before they get a chance to leave you.

- You fear being alone, and surround yourself with people all the time.

- You keep friends at a distance, or push them away before they can disappoint you.

- You give too much.

- You are extremely private and cagey.

- You question whether your partner or friends really love you.

- You have difficulty generating feelings of closeness or intimacy.

The abandonment wound leaves you constantly on edge, facing a frightening world on your own. *Do whatever you can to please the tribe!* your brain might yell. Or, *Don't bother joining a tribe, they'll just leave you anyway!* You might become overly self-reliant, a lonesome cowboy traversing the desert on his own, never letting anyone get too close; or you may become a gushing debutante, falling all over yourself to win people over, while losing touch with who you really are and what you really value. Let's look at a few of these symptoms in more detail.

Not Being Vulnerable with Others

A client came to me because he was having trouble opening his heart in a relationship. He had finally met somebody he could imagine spending the rest of his life with, but he felt that he was holding back. He described the sensation of a physical barrier over his heart, like a thick piece of leather. This barrier had been there ever since his mother died of cancer when he was nine years old, an event that had completely shattered his childhood.

He and his brother had been sent to live with an aunt and uncle who were already overwhelmed by the demands of their own children. Nobody was available to help him manage his pain, grief, and confusion. He had been very close with his mother, but now he closed his heart. He didn't understand why *his* mother had died, when his friends' and cousins' mothers were still alive. Like many children, he assumed that her death had something to do with him—that she had abandoned him because he wasn't worth sticking around for.

Now that he had found the partner of his dreams, these feelings of inadequacy were coming back with a vengeance. He felt that he had to work very hard to keep his partner interested, and anticipate their every need, or else they would leave. At the same time, he was terrified of showing his true self to his partner, or expressing a full range of emotions. He tried to create a "perfect" self to show his partner in the hopes that this would protect him from abandonment, but meanwhile he was withholding the vulnerability that relationships require to thrive.

Leaving Others Before They Can Leave You

Another client of mine found it easy to find romantic partners, and enjoyed the falling-in-love phase very much—but when her partners started talking about commitments such as moving in together or having children, she would find a reason to break up with them. These breakups were often very sudden. She blindsided her partners with the news that she no longer wanted to be with them—and that was that, relationship over.

Although she longed to get married and have children, she couldn't seem to stop this pattern of breaking off connections as soon as commitment seemed imminent. As the prospect of happiness seemed more and more likely, so did the prospect of getting hurt. Her response was to abandon her partner before they could do the thing she most feared—which was to abandon *her*.

As a child, her parents had left her with her grandparents in Thailand while they emigrated to the United States for work. Although they had promised to send for her once they were established, this had never come to pass. She grew up feeling like she'd been left behind. In her adult life, she craved closeness and stability, without realizing the ways in which she herself was sabotaging her hopes of getting these things. She was blind, also, to the ways in which her abrupt manner of breaking off relationships was injuring others in the exact same way she had been injured as a child.

Constantly Seeking Reassurance

The abandonment wound can show up as a need for frequent reassurance that you are loved and valued, combined with anxiously scanning for signs that another abandonment is imminent.

I had a client who was ten years old when her father walked out on the family. She was absolutely blindsided—one day, he was there, and the next day he was gone, leaving no note and providing no explanation. She later found out that he had moved across the country to be with a woman he'd met online. Although her father had been warm and loving—or perhaps *because* he had been warm and loving—his departure made her question her entire reality. Suddenly, she wasn't sure if he had ever really loved her, her mother, and her siblings after all. Maybe she had read him wrong.

This wound had a profound impact on her day-to-day life long after she'd grown up and gotten married herself. Every day when she came home from work, she felt a prickle of anxiety as she wondered whether or not her husband would still be there. She called him several times a day just to hear his voice, and paid close attention to any small changes in his mood or his schedule. If he seemed a little bit distracted or preoccupied, it could trigger an emotional meltdown in her as she began to worry that he was about to leave.

He sometimes complained that he was endlessly having to prove his love to her. No matter how faithful, dependable, and present he was, she was always seeking more reassurance that he really loved her and intended to stay. This anxiety was straining the relationship to the point that it risked becoming a self-fulfilling prophecy. "I feel like I'm always on trial," he told her, "and that's no way to live. *You're* the one who needs to decide to trust me—nothing I can do will make you feel OK."

Risks of the Abandonment Wound

Left untreated, abandonment wounds can cause you to drive away the people closest to you. They can keep you in a constant cycle of seeking approval, as you try to find solid ground by gaining favor with other people. They can even cause you to abandon others, because you assume that your presence is not really valued and therefore will not be missed if you leave.

The good news is, you can heal your abandonment wound and free yourself from its painful patterns. In the next chapter, I will share my favorite tools for doing exactly that.

Part 1

Healing Practices

If the abandonment wound is caused when an unwritten contract is broken—for example, "Parents look after their children"—it begins to heal when we make *new* contracts with life and with ourselves. My own abandonment wound began to heal when I made the contract to always give and receive love. I did this by smiling at others, petting dogs and holding babies, painting pictures, singing, letting my friends know how much they meant to me, and letting myself know how much *I* meant to me.

What are some other contracts we can make with life? How about "I am worthy—even if this romantic partner decides not to be with me," or "I belong—even if I'm not 100 percent perfect all the time."

As we establish these new contracts with life, our capacity for connection deepens. We stop fearing abandonment, and learn to enjoy the messy, weird, surprising, difficult, and rewarding process of letting other people into our lives.

I once worked with a client who was highly accomplished—and incredibly stern. The first time we met, I was struck by her coldness and rigidity. After speaking with her for a while, it emerged that she had been raised by parents who were constantly absent. Her father traveled frequently and was rarely home, and her mother worked long hours and was emotionally unavailable. She was left alone a lot even as a toddler, and when her sister was born three years later, my client was put in charge of her.

By age seven, she was responsible for making meals not only for herself but also for her sister and younger brother. She did this so well that her parents praised her for her competence—then gave her *more* responsibilities. As a result of her precocity, she ended up essentially raising herself and her younger siblings.

At the time we started working together, she was the CEO of a marketing company. At home, everybody knew her as the "trigger finger," because she would immediately get triggered when somebody she cared about wasn't available. For example, if she called her son at university and he didn't call back right away, she would get very upset—either weeping or flying into a rage. Although she'd never been able to express her anger at her parents for abandoning her as a child, she felt "safe" expressing it toward her husband and children—even though they had done little to deserve it.

As part of our work together, she made some new agreements, among them, "I can love and care for myself, even when the person I want to be with isn't available. And I trust that my husband and children love me, no matter how upset I feel." When she got triggered, she learned to stop and practice self-care instead of lashing out at whoever was nearby. In other words, she stopped abandoning herself, and started providing herself with the love and soothing she should have had all along. Her abandonment wound began to heal, and she felt happier and more at ease, knowing that she could take care of her difficult emotions on the inside without damaging her relationships with her husband and sons.

The pain of abandonment can feel overpowering, but by slowly and steadily opening ourselves to love, we can defuse its energy. No matter how small or worthless an experience of abandonment has made you feel, you can rebuild a sense of self-worth by refusing to abandon yourself, even in the midst of difficult emotions. You can give yourself the love and care you always needed—and in so doing, attract more of it into your life from other sources.

Healing Practice: Discovering the Love of Your Life

One of my favorite spiritual teachers, don Jose Ruiz, speaks about the importance of realizing that you are the love of your life. He says that even though you may have a spouse or romantic partner, your first responsibility is to nourish and protect the one being who has been permanently entrusted to your care—you!

If you were abandoned or neglected as a child, you may not have had the skills or knowledge required to take good care of yourself. Indeed, even as an adult, self-care may not come easily to you (after all, when were you supposed to learn those skills, and from who?). But no matter how awkward or unfamiliar it may feel to take good care of yourself, you can learn those skills starting today.

A client of mine had been neglected as a child, and often went to school in mismatched clothes, without enough to eat. As an adult, she often went days without brushing her hair, and was chronically underweight because it simply didn't occur to her to eat. She put little thought into her appearance, and used clothes simply as way to cover her body. Although she saw that other people enjoyed expressing themselves through their clothes and taking care of their bodies, this had never felt like an option to her—indeed, these things almost felt forbidden.

I sensed that this seeming obliviousness to her own needs was a kind of repetition trauma—a way of repeating the original neglect, carrying it forward into her adult life. In failing to brush her hair or respond appropriately to her body's hunger cues, she was showing herself the same neglect her parents had shown her. I suggested that, for a period of two weeks, she do an experiment. What would happen if she let herself do all of those "forbidden" acts of care for herself—including things that felt outrageous, like getting a haircut, or buying a pair of pants that fit properly?

Although she struggled with feelings of anxiety when she "wasted" time brushing her hair in the morning, and worried that it was vain to wear flattering clothes, my client carried out the experiment successfully. She realized that she felt better when she was clean, well groomed, and not half-starved—she'd just never believed that she, like everyone else, was worthy of those things. Although she had been abandoned as a child, she no longer chose to abandon herself. She could, and did, learn the new skills required to take good care of the love of her life.

What are three things you can start doing to take care of the love of *your* life? Write them on a sticky note and place it on your fridge or some other prominent place in your home. Can you treat yourself like someone worth caring for? What happens when you move from neglecting yourself to cherishing yourself?

Healing Practice: Practicing Time Traveling

The human imagination is very powerful. Our brains can't always tell the difference between "real" experiences and ones that we have merely imagined in detail. This is a downside a lot of the time, because if you sit around having anxious thoughts about imaginary scenarios, it's the same physiologically as if they actually happened. On the other hand, you can harness this power for good by imagining positive, healing scenarios.

What if you could travel back in time to the day you were abandoned? What if your current self could swoop in like a superhero and help out the version of you who experienced the abandonment? What would you do for that person? How would you help them? What needs would you fulfill? What would have been the ideal response?

For example, if you were abandoned by a parent, you might imagine yourself stepping in to take care of your child self—cooking for her, getting her school clothes ready in the morning, and doing all the things that would ideally have been done for you when you were abandoned. Imagine these things in as much detail as possible—really treat it like you've been given a chance to rewrite your own history. Even if you can't change the facts of the abandonment itself, you can still give yourself the love and care you needed.

Next, write this new and improved story down in your journal. Here's my version:

> After my mom left me and my sister with our grandmother and went to Europe, grown-up Marie came and talked to us. "I know this hurts right now," she said. "But you have to believe me, it isn't personal. Your mom didn't leave you because you're bad kids or unworthy—she left because of her own wounds. You girls are treasures. You are beautiful, smart, and funny. You deserve all the love and protection in the world, and I am here to give you that. I will always stick around, no matter what—in fact, you can't get rid of me, even if you try!"

Whenever your abandonment wound is feeling sore, you can go back and visit your inner child in this way, giving her the love and reassurance she needs.

Healing Practice: Writing a Letter from Your Abandoner

This is another practice that involves the imagination. Even though the person or persons who abandoned you may be long gone, or may never explain or apologize for their actions, you can still give yourself the experience of receiving an apology or explanation by using your imagination. In an ideal world, what would this person say to you? In an ideal world, what would they do to make amends? It doesn't matter if this will never happen in real life—you can get most of the benefits just by imagining it.

Write yourself a letter from the point of view of the person who abandoned you. In this letter, write all the things you would most like to hear from this person—why they did it, how sorry they are, and so forth.

Here is an example from a client of mine whose husband abandoned her:

Dear Judy,

I am so sorry for walking out on you and the kids all those years ago. I can't imagine how much pain that must have caused you, and how confused and hurt you must have felt. You were counting on me for so many things—to be a father to the kids, and a partner to you, and even basic things like fixing the sink and paying my share of the mortgage. I left you holding the bag, and there's no excuse for that.

At the time I left, I told myself that you were so strong and capable that you'd be just fine without me. I am ashamed now to think of the ways I deluded myself to make my actions seem OK. You deserved so much more than what I gave you, and I am so, so sorry.

Sincerely,

Ron

By writing this letter, you can give yourself a real experience of healing and validation, even if the person who abandoned you never apologizes or explains. By using your imagination, you take back some of your power, and cut the energetic cords tying you to the situation.

Healing Practice: Imagining Your Ideal Relationship

Many people with abandonment wounds struggle with intimate relationships, myself included. Either we pull people in too close, clinging to them for fear of letting them out of our sights, or we keep them at a distance, wary of letting them get close enough to hurt us. Both of these strategies can result in finding yourself single when you don't want to be, or stuck in unfulfilling relationships again and again.

We tend to get the kinds of relationships we expect to have—in part because, as a participant in the relationship, we recreate the patterns we know; but also because we unconsciously attract partners who meet our expectations. With this in mind, we can shift our relationships by consciously imagining what we want, instead of letting our unconscious patterns steer the ship.

For this healing exercise, imagine the kind of romantic relationship you'd like to have. Write it down in the present tense, as if you already have it. Here's an example:

> My partner always lets me know what's on his mind, and I don't worry about stumbling over some emotional landmine I didn't realize was there. I feel a deep sense of security

and mutual understanding, and these feelings are justified because my partner is trustworthy and communicates well. I feel calm and happy throughout the day. I know that I am perfectly loveable. My partner and I have a good mix of togetherness and independence, and we can be apart for short periods comfortably, knowing we will reconnect joyfully later on.

By writing down exactly what you want, you are telling the universe you are ready to receive it. Not only that, but you are clarifying what is desirable for you in a relationship, as opposed to what you'd merely accept. The next time you find yourself in a relationship, you can refer to what you've written, checking to see how closely it correlates with the ideals you've stated.

Signs Your Abandonment Wound Is Healing

As your abandonment wound begins to heal, you will find that your relationships become much easier. Instead of scanning for signs of imminent abandonment, you can fully enjoy the present moment. Instead of running yourself ragged trying to please people, you can be yourself, knowing that you'll be fine whether or not everybody likes you. You will start to move through the world with a sense of confidence and security, knowing that you have a powerful ally in your own self.

Paradoxically, this newfound strength will make it much easier for you to be vulnerable with others. Knowing that you are fundamentally secure makes it possible to reveal your weaknesses, which is essential for forming emotionally close friendships and relationships. When their abandonment wounds begin to heal, my clients often report better sleep, less pain in their bodies, and an overall reduction in anxiety—not just anxiety related to abandonment. They know they are safe within themselves, and their entire body seems to relax in response.

Here are some key signs that your abandonment wound is healing:

- You find it easier to trust other people.

- You find it easier to practice self-care.

- Your inner voice has become gentler and more supportive.

- You feel valued and loved by others, without needing explicit reassurance of these facts.

- You detect the love in others' actions easily.

- You feel comfortable expressing your true preferences and opinions.

- You feel comfortable receiving, not only giving.

- You feel a sense of loyalty toward others and do not abandon them.

- You feel comfortable alone or in the company of others.

Hidden Treasure: Connection

When your abandonment wound starts to heal, the treasure of connection will reveal itself. You will realize that even in the midst of your worst abandonment, your capacity for connection was still there, waiting to be reactivated. By practicing self-care, you establish a loving relationship with yourself that will sustain you regardless of who else comes in and out of your life. By tending to your inner child, you can fill yourself with the loving energy that was cut off when you were first abandoned. By making peace with the person who originally abandoned or neglected you, you assert that you are bigger than the abandonment. And by joyfully affirming your relationship ideals, you attract secure, loving connection into your life.

Part 2

The Betrayal Wound

After my father took me and my sister to live with him when I was seven years old, we had to adapt to a whole new home and family—including a stepmother and stepsiblings who weren't exactly happy to welcome us into their lives. My stepmother was like the stepmother of fairy tales: cruel, cold, and intensely jealous of the affection my father had for us. As for my stepsiblings, they missed no opportunity to tease us or even hit us.

When I went to my father for comfort and protection, he was quick to brush off my distress: Of course my stepmother loved me! I was just being dramatic. Maybe if I were just a little nicer to my stepsiblings we would get along just fine. Other times, he would appease me by promising to talk to my stepmother about the problem, or he would suggest that we take a special trip to the zoo or the beach together—just him, my sister, and me. Yet, at the last minute, he'd invite my stepmother and stepsiblings to come along—conveniently making it impossible for us to talk to him about what was going on.

These betrayals were crushing. Even at seven years old, I could tell that my father was keeping himself willfully ignorant of the depth of my despair. He didn't want to deal with the raw, messy work of integrating the two families he'd created, so instead he was leaving me and my sister to fend for ourselves in a hostile new environment. I was hurt and outraged. How could he pretend not to see what was going on? How could he throw me under the bus and, worse, imply that I was exaggerating, when he was supposed to protect me? My trust in him was shattered. It was devastating to realize that I couldn't count on him—that he would, in fact, betray me in order to make his own life easier.

As an adult, I kept finding myself drawn to men who never had enough time for me, and who were always changing our plans to include other people. For example, I once dated a man who insisted on bringing his best friend along on nearly all of our activities. When we went out for dinner, the friend would come; when we went for a hike, the friend would be there. This man and I could never talk about the serious issues in our relationship because his friend was always there, acting as a natural buffer against intimacy—the same way my father had invited his new wife and children to come to the zoo with us, so that my sister and I never had the chance to tell him how we really felt.

Just like my father, the men I dated also tended to throw me under the bus when they got stressed out or overwhelmed. For example, one guy I dated would leave me to entertain guests that he had invited over—I would find him in his bedroom playing computer games, while I'd been struggling to think of things to say to his friends for the last hour. Although this might sound funny, it was actually a pretty big betrayal for an introvert like me who hadn't wanted company in the first place.

It was only after deep self-examination that I realized these patterns were due to my betrayal wound. Although my mind had stopped thinking about how badly my father had hurt me long ago, the effects were showing up in my emotions, in my body, and in my behavior.

Discovering even a "minor" betrayal can turn your world upside down. It forces you to reassess everything you thought was true, and reevaluate relationships that may have previously felt secure. At its mildest, betrayal can be awkward; for example, a teacher who catches a student cheating will still need to interact with that student for the rest of the year. The largest betrayals—things like a spouse cheating or a trusted employee embezzling money—can be completely devastating, severing longstanding relationships and exploding entire families or social networks, and leading to enduring trauma for the person betrayed.

A client of mine confided in her friend about some trouble she was going through with her partner. A few days later, she ran into an acquaintance at the gym who inquired about the very problems she had asked her friend to keep confidential. Realizing that her friend had talked about her situation to a third party was deeply troubling for my client. She wondered what other intimate information her friend had divulged to people for whom it wasn't intended. Her sense of trust and ease in the relationship were replaced by doubt and awkwardness. She felt angry and betrayed, and at the same time, she mourned the loss of the ideal friendship she'd believed she had. Her disappointment over this loss was even more crushing than the initial betrayal.

We've all experienced some level of betrayal at some point in our lives. Depending on the depth of the betrayal, you may find yourself going over the events again and again, trying to figure out where you missed the signs, or how you might have prevented the betrayal from happening. You may even consciously or unconsciously try to find a way the betrayal is your fault, because that is slightly less painful than sitting with the awareness that another human has hurt or disappointed you. You may feel a deep sense of shame for allowing yourself to be betrayed, or feel a painful sense of exposure if the betrayal becomes public knowledge. Worst of all, you may feel that the world has become scary and unfamiliar overnight, with all your points of reference thrown into question. It can take a long time to regain a sense of solidity and security both within yourself and in your relationships with others.

Origins of the Betrayal Wound

The betrayal wound can have its origins in any experience that shatters your trust in a person who is or was important to you—whether that's a family member, a friend, a teacher, a spiritual leader, a romantic partner or spouse, or a boss, employee, or coworker. Betrayal can also take place within the context of an institution. For example, as an adult you may experience profound betrayal when the company to which you've been loyal for twenty years eliminates your job, or when the members of a community group with which you're involved turn against you.

Here are just a handful of experiences that can leave you with a betrayal wound:

- Being lied to, or being forced to participate in a lie

- Being physically, sexually, or emotionally abused, especially by a parent, family member, or other trusted adult

- Being promised things that never come to pass

- Having the promise of love or intimacy dangled in front of you and repeatedly yanked away

- Having your own legitimate claim on a parent or caregiver's attention repeatedly bypassed in favor of somebody or something else

- Giving your all to a person or institution, only to be insulted or taken advantage of

- Catching a person you esteem highly in an immoral act, whether or not it affects you personally

The betrayal wound permanently alters your relationship with the person or institution who betrayed you. Although you may forgive that person, you will never recapture the state of innocence that existed when you first trusted them, and you may find it much more difficult to trust others in the future. In that sense, betrayal doesn't just injure one relationship—it injures *all* of your relationships. This is why it's so important to pay careful attention to this wound.

Signs You Are Living with a Betrayal Wound

If you were betrayed at a very young age, you may not remember the details of the incident. However, your body still absorbed the profound violation of the betrayal, and your ability to trust others was still impacted. For example, one of my clients was frequently yelled at and terrorized by her father before he left the family when she was three. Although she could not remember his rages, she held them in her body in the form of muscular tension, and in her emotional body in the form of defensiveness and distrust.

If you are living with a betrayal wound, you might notice these kinds of patterns:

- You avoid asking people for help or favors because you don't trust them to follow through.

- You avoid confiding in people because you believe they may expose you in some way.

- You double-check other people's work because you don't trust them to do it properly.

- You make backup plans to preemptively deal with being let down.

- You become cynical about humanity: "All men are pigs," "women are bitches," etc.

- You are plagued with doubts/suspicions and prone to drawing conclusions indicating betrayal: "She's five minutes late—she must be with someone else."

- You are overly naive and gullible, and fail to exercise reasonable caution with people or situations: "But I just walked away from my purse for a minute . . ." "He told me he'd pay me back as soon as his check came in . . ."

- You betray others before they have a chance to betray you.

- You avoid interacting with people or forming close relationships.

- You engage in chronic busyness, overwork, and self-distraction.

- You experience depression, anxiety, and loneliness.

The betrayal wound can be hard to recognize, especially if your coping strategies are valued by the outside world. For example, your family may applaud you for your work ethic, not realizing that your extreme focus on work is a way to avoid forming close relationships. People may respect you for your "emotional control," not realizing that this springs from an inability to trust others with your most vulnerable self. It can take some careful searching to recognize all the ways the betrayal wound is active in your life. My clients are often surprised to discover to what extent a betrayal has affected their entire manner of living and relating.

Here are some of the most common ways I've seen the betrayal wound show up:

Having Difficulty Determining Who Is Trustworthy

Being betrayed can push your risk-assessment instruments out of calibration, so that you either wildly overestimate your risk of being betrayed by anyone and everyone, or underestimate the risk. For example, you might repeatedly put your trust in people who really shouldn't be trusted, ignoring the signs that they are going to betray you. On the other extreme, you might repeatedly fail to trust people who *are* trustworthy, isolating yourself and cutting off needed support.

One client of mine grew up with an alcoholic father who was forever making promises and then breaking them. For example, one year he told her over and over how excited he was to see her perform in the school Christmas pageant, and even promised to take her out for french fries and hot cocoa after the performance. But when the big night arrived, he was at the bar getting drunk—he didn't even remember the promises he had made.

As an adult, my client was constantly getting involved with boyfriends who promised to do things with her, and were forever letting her down. Many of these boyfriends were substance users, just like her father had been. No matter how many times this process repeated itself, my client couldn't seem to see that as long as they had untreated addictions, these men would *always* break their promises and fail to show up for her in the ways she needed. She chronically underestimated the likelihood of being betrayed as a way of protecting herself from the pain this wound had caused her. She was overly optimistic about the men she dated and overconfident in her predictions about their behavior. Although her female friends were trustworthy and reliable, she had trouble properly assessing the character of men.

Experiencing Extreme Self-Doubt

If you placed your trust in someone who later betrayed you, your self-confidence can take a serious hit. If you were wrong once, how can you ever come to trust your own judgment again? You might blame yourself for trusting the person who betrayed you, or beat yourself up for being naive, gullible, or failing to read the signs. You might fall into a deep depression in which the world comes to seem like a harsh, inhospitable place, and relationships with other humans feel dangerous and fraught; you might feel a deep sense of grief, loss, and even fear.

A client of mine had been cheated by her business partner when she was in her early thirties. The two of them had been friends since college, and had founded a successful real estate agency together. But two years into the partnership, my client discovered that her partner had been diverting money into a secret account. This discovery shattered her world. Not only were there complicated financial issues to resolve, which was stressful enough in its own right, but the sense of joyful teamwork she'd enjoyed with her business partner now felt false. She found herself reevaluating every little interaction she'd had with her friend since founding the business. It felt like all the happiness she'd experienced over the past two years was getting sucked down a drain, replaced by ugliness, anger, and confusion.

Although she was still the same intelligent, self-motivated person she'd been before the betrayal, the incident left her mired in crippling doubt that extended to all areas of her life. Not only was she unsure who she could trust going forward, but she was suddenly questioning her ability to run a business, have a career, or even decide what to eat for dinner that night. Nothing felt right anymore—everything felt saturated with uncertainty and the potential for chaos. Her life began to collapse around this state of paralyzing doubt.

Overfunctioning

If you've been betrayed by someone who was supposed to take care of you, you may come to the conclusion that the only person on whom you can ever rely is yourself. Not only that, but you may doubt other people's ability to take care of their own lives, and believe that you are literally the only reliable person around.

This can manifest as overfunctioning: taking on the emotions, problems, and responsibilities of the people around you. Although you may be very on the ball yourself, you might unconsciously seek out partners who are disorganized, irresponsible, or scatter-brained, and then take on the task of making their lives work.

A client of mine was sexually abused by his step-father when he was a young boy. Although he told his mother of the abuse, she made the decision to stay with the abuser. In other words, she chose to pre-serve that relationship over her relationship with her son. This betrayal was devastating to my client. He learned that *nobody* had the courage or competence to protect him—he had to protect himself. He began working as soon as he was legally able, around age fourteen, and moved out of the house before he'd finished high school. He put himself through medi-cal school, working nearly around the clock, and became a successful doctor.

In addition to working and paying off his stu-dent loans, he spent long hours helping out his high school friends who were considerably less success-ful than he was—driving one of them around to look at apartments, counseling another through a stint in rehab. He frequently took in friends, then cooked and cleaned for them and helped them look for jobs, never pausing to consider if his friends might be capa-ble of doing these things for themselves. His experi-ence of betrayal had left him with the illusion that he alone was competent, not only to run his own life, but to run the lives of his friends. He fell into similar patterns at work, taking on tasks that belonged to the nurses, assistants, and even receptionists.

In our work together, we spent a lot of time exploring the feelings of anxiety that came up for him when he contemplated allowing other people to carry out their own tasks. He realized that not only was he trying to protect himself from the disappointment he would feel if they failed, he was trying to protect others from the shame of failing. He sensed that, although she had a hard time expressing it, his mother was ashamed of her failure to intervene on his behalf; and at an unconscious level he saw it as his job to protect her from these feelings of shame.

Risks of the Betrayal Wound

Left untreated, a betrayal wound can rob you of opportunities to be truly intimate with other people. By trusting the wrong people, or refraining from trusting anyone at all, you miss out on the wonderful sense of security that comes from being part of a resilient web of social relationships. You wander around in a state of bafflement, wondering why you keep getting hurt—or you become jaded and cynical, expecting the worst from everyone at all times.

In extreme cases, the betrayal wound can cause you to chronically betray others. You may find yourself lying, cheating, gossiping, or making false promises simply because this is what you've been conditioned to see as normal. You may believe that doing these things is what's necessary to get ahead in the world, and do untold damage to your relationships in the process. Luckily, the betrayal wound *can* be healed. I will share my favorite tools for doing that in the next chapter.

Part 2

Healing Practices

Healing the betrayal wound involves fully feeling the emotions evoked by the experience of betrayal, no matter how far in the past the original betrayal may be. Feeling the emotions associated with betrayal can be difficult. Not only can they be very uncomfortable, but for many of us, they can feel taboo. If the person who betrayed you is a relative, spiritual leader, or other person you've been socialized to love and respect, it can be nearly impossible to allow yourself to feel the full scope of your rage, disgust, and disappointment. Even if the betrayal was perpetrated by a stranger, it can be so unpleasant to feel these emotions that we choose to bury them or gloss over them instead.

For me, this process started by naming my emotions. I wasn't sure how I felt about my father's behavior—so I asked! *Am I furious? Do I want to take revenge? Do I feel humiliated? Am I ashamed that this happened to me?* By making these inquiries with curiosity, I slowly gained access to the emotions I'd repressed. I found out that I was angry at my father, and I did indeed feel humiliated by the ways he'd swept my concerns under the rug when I was young.

If you have a hard time identifying your emotions, you might want to look at the following list to see which ones resonate for you:

- Anger

- Anxiety

- Bafflement

- Confusion

- Disappointment

- Disgust

- Embarrassment

- Fear

- Hurt

- Regret

- Resentment

- Shame

- Sorrow

As you read over this list of emotions, pay close attention to your body's response. Do you feel nauseous? Is your jaw clenched? Are your palms sweating? Are you tearing up? These are signs that the emotion in question is indeed lurking just out of your awareness.

Pay attention to these physical sensations. Allow them to intensify, while remaining within your window of tolerance. Give yourself plenty of time to experience these emotions however they manifest for you. For example, you might need to cry, shake, swear, or just stare into space for a while. There is no need to "fix" these emotions or change them in any way; just experience them as fully as you are able.

Once you have fully experienced the emotions associated with the betrayal, the next step in healing this wound is to put anger and blame in their proper place. Many of my clients with betrayal wounds have turned their anger inward, blaming themselves for the betrayal and cursing themselves for being "stupid" or "naive." Even when a betrayal is extremely clear-cut, such as an act of violence, we still have a tendency to look for ways it was our fault.

For example, a client of mine had been raped by her brother's friend. Although she had plenty of anger about this awful event, it was mostly directed at herself—she told herself she shouldn't have gone to the New Year's Eve party, she shouldn't have drunk champagne, and so forth. It was actually very difficult for her to feel anger toward the man who raped her, because that would mean facing the painful truth that another human being had knowingly and intentionally harmed her. Our work together consisted of building a container in which she felt safe enough to finally allow her rage at the perpetrator to come through.

Some people cope with betrayal by denying it happened at all. This is especially common among children who must hide the truth of abuse from themselves in order to preserve their relationship with an abusive caregiver, but it can also be true in romantic relationships or in relationships with powerful institutions such as schools and places of employment. When your survival depends on a specific person or institution, you are incentivized to ignore wrongdoing, and this apparent complicity can make the betrayal wound even more difficult to untangle.

Another way I see clients coping with betrayal wounds is by minimizing and downplaying the severity of an event. "Everything is fine, I'm fine," they might say. "It wasn't that big a deal." We try to make the wound smaller by dismissing it, turning it into a joke, or conjuring up a hard shell for ourselves. For example, an adult who was neglected as a child might tell "funny" stories about having too little to eat, or wearing dirty clothes for days on end, while guarding themselves against the real pain of being betrayed by their caregivers. A person who was betrayed by a colleague might say, "It's a dog-eat-dog world," as if it were normal to steal another person's work, sabotage a promotion, or otherwise act in an unscrupulous way.

There is nothing wrong with using humor to defuse difficult emotions, or doing your best not to take a betrayal personally. However, it's important to make sure that in doing so, you're not bypassing the all-important work of healing the wound. If you find yourself making light of an event that could reasonably be expected to hurt someone, ask yourself, *Have I grieved this? If this happened to a friend of mine, would I be shrugging it off in a similar way?*

Healing Practice: Writing a Betrayal Letter

If you've been denying, minimizing, or taking inappropriate responsibility for another person's betrayal, try writing that person a letter in which you take inventory of all the ways the betrayal affected you. You don't have to send the letter—the goal is to become aware of the full scope of the betrayal, and to help yourself realize that it would be normal and reasonable for you to feel hurt by it.

For example, you might write, "Dear Sheila, ever since you plagiarized my work, I've been having a hard time trusting other people. I feel unmotivated to carry on with my research, because I'm plagued by a sense it will just be stolen from me. I feel cynical and depressed about the entire field of academia to which I've devoted my life and which used to be a source of joy and stimulation to me."

As you take inventory of all the ways the betrayal has affected your life, allow yourself to feel whatever emotions well up. Don't be surprised if this thorough accounting of the betrayal's effects causes you to feel grief, anger, or powerlessness, especially if you've never let yourself experience those feelings before. It is only by experiencing the pain of this wound that you can begin to heal it.

Healing Practice: Writing a Forgiveness Letter to Yourself

In addition to fully feeling your anger toward the person who betrayed you, healing the betrayal wound can also involve acknowledging any residual anger toward yourself. In this variation on the betrayal letter practice, you write a letter to yourself, releasing yourself of any lingering blame or shame you hold around the betrayal event.

For example, you might write, "Dear [Your Name], I'm so sorry I blamed you for the abuse you experienced. I can see now that none of it was your fault, and you were only doing the best you could to survive. I know now that everything you did came out of a desire to protect me, and a wish to see the best in other people. I release you from all guilt, shame, and self-blame concerning this event."

As you write, allow any feelings of grief and sorrow to bubble up and be felt. You may also feel a sense of relief as you finally release yourself from a burden that was never yours to begin with.

If you have found a sense of security in blaming yourself for the betrayal, this self-forgiveness practice can bring up feelings of extreme vulnerability. Go slowly, and practice self-care: stop if you become overwhelmed, and engage in a grounding practice such as stretching, walking, or talking with a trusted friend.

Healing Practice: Taking Inventory

If your betrayal wound has caused you to doubt your ability to assess people and situations, it can be helpful to take a clear look at the person you were when the betrayal happened as compared with the person you are now. Many people who have experienced betrayal develop a fear of making the same mistake again, and doing this practice can help you identify the ways in which you have already become less likely to fall for the tactics that harmed you in the past.

For example, my client who was cheated by her business partner wrote the following list describing her former and current selves:

Person I Was Then	Person I Am Now
Starry-eyed	Several years of business experience
Trusting	Not afraid to ask for proof or double-check what people say
Inexperienced at running a business	Well versed in financial and legal matters
Eager to please; afraid of conflict/ making waves	Experienced with handling conflict
Inexperienced at setting boundaries	Able to recognize red flags in other people

After my client wrote these two lists, she realized all the ways she'd grown and changed since her experience of betrayal. At thirty-seven, she would never end up in the same situation as she did when she was thirty-one. For one thing, she was older and wiser and had more life experience. But the experience of betrayal had also forced her to grow in key ways, both in the practical sense of running a business, and in the emotional sense of setting boundaries, facing conflict head-on, and having better radar for when other people are acting shady. Writing these lists gave her a newfound sense of confidence. Her self-doubt began to fade, and she went on to have a successful career.

Healing Practice: Honoring Your Deep Needs

We often allow ourselves to be betrayed when we need something very badly. For example, a boy who is being bullied at school might continue to ingratiate himself with his tormentors, because the need to be accepted by other kids is so strong. A woman who conveniently fails to notice her husband's cheating might be driven by a need to give her children the "intact" home she never had herself. A meditation student who is betrayed by a teacher or guru might ignore that person's misbehavior because they have a deep need to believe that *someone* out there is holy and pure.

What were the deep needs driving your own willingness to overlook the betrayal you experienced? Were you longing for an ideal friendship or romantic relationship? For love and belonging? A sense of security? Or bare survival? Do you have a deep need to be seen as good, loyal, forgiving, or dependable? As you ponder these questions, write the answers down in your journal. Here's one example:

> At the time my boyfriend cheated on me, I had a deep need to be in a relationship, period. In my mind, it was better to have a cheating boyfriend than no boyfriend at all. I thought that being in a relationship, any relationship, automatically raised my status, whereas being single made me feel like I was a loser ("on the shelf," as my mother would say). Now, I can see that my need for a relationship to validate my existence caused me to be willfully blind to the many ways my boyfriend betrayed me, not just his cheating.

Getting in touch with your deepest needs and desires can protect you against being taken advantage of again. For example, my client with the alcoholic father had to constantly forgive his bad behavior in order to preserve their relationship. In her adult life, she had unconsciously maintained this pattern of forgiving unacceptable behavior because she believed that this was a normal and necessary part of being in a relationship at all. Once she saw this pattern for what it was, she started to set better boundaries with the men she dated, and she stopped experiencing so much betrayal in her intimate relationships.

Signs Your Betrayal Wound Is Healing

In my adult life, my own betrayal wound manifested as extreme defensiveness. I felt that I couldn't trust anybody, and so I was quick to anger at even the most benign interactions.

For example, I always got very edgy when I went to a party or social event and people would ask me whether I was married or had children. I always felt I had to launch into a justification of my life choices, explaining that I was in medical school and then residency, working so many hours a day with no time to maintain an intimate relationship. In my mind, the only reason people had to ask me these questions was so they could gossip about me later—*Marie is nearly thirty-five years old and still no husband—can you imagine?*

As I began to heal from my betrayal wound, I noticed this anger and defensiveness in a new way. I realized that I automatically assumed that when people asked me this question, they were trying to shame me for my relationship status. I took the question as an attack, and responded with an intensity befitting an attack. But as my wound began to heal, I thought, *Wait a minute. Maybe they're not asking this question to shame me—maybe they want to know if I'm already married, because if not, they want to set me up with their cute cousin. Maybe they want to know if I have kids, because they want to make me an auntie to their kids.*

It occurred to me there were all kinds of reasons people might ask me these questions, but as long as I'd been living in my betrayal wound, I could only assume the worst motivations. Maybe the other person was going to say, "You're not married? Good for you! I *am* married and my husband never puts the toilet seat down." The wound had become a filter through which I saw reality, and as it healed, that filter began to widen so that more positive interpretations could come through.

Your betrayal wound is healing if you notice any of the following things:

- A newfound willingness to trust others

- A willingness to confront others for bad behavior

- A decrease in hypervigilance

- Feelings of calm and centeredness

- The ability to feel and express appropriate anger

- An end of "repetition" behaviors such as getting into the same type of relationship again and again

- A sense of ease and health in the body

- A sense of mental clarity; an end of ruminations and second-guessing; better decision-making ability

- An increased sense of self-confidence

Hidden Treasure: Wisdom

As the shadow of betrayal begins to lift, the treasure of wisdom is revealed in its wake. When we successfully process and release a betrayal wound, we emerge wiser in every sense of the word. We are more discerning in our relationships, more skilled at navigating institutions, and more attuned to our intuition. We know when to give people and institutions a second chance, and when to cut ties. We trust ourselves to make sound judgments, knowing that we are coming from a place of clarity, experience, and knowledge.

Wisdom allows us say no when we encounter a person who is likely to hurt us, but also say yes when we encounter a person who is worthy of our trust.

It helps us build appropriate walls to keep us secure from those who would take advantage of us, but also tear down the walls that are keeping us from enjoying deep and loving connections with safe and benevolent others. With our wisdom as our guide, we can make appropriate choices about who we let in and who we keep out, and welcome secure, trustworthy relationships into our lives.

Part 3

The Denial Wound

When I was fourteen years old, my mother became sick with cancer. Although she had been absent for most of my childhood, I nevertheless felt a deep sense of loyalty toward her, and I craved her love and approval. As part of her treatment for cancer, she decided to work with Iboga—a powerful plant medicine used by traditional healers in Cameroon. Iboga is a small evergreen shrub that is native to Central Africa. When prepared by an experienced healer, the bark produces powerful visions that can last for hours.

Although my mother was determined to work with Iboga, she was too weak from the cancer to take the medicine herself. The adults decided that I should take it on her behalf, as a kind of surrogate—a decision that would change my life forever.

At fourteen years old, I wasn't really prepared for the intensity of the Iboga experience. I had never taken any kind of psychedelic substance before—I'd never even gotten drunk. But suddenly, I had to ingest a substance that transported me to an entirely different reality. Within thirty minutes of taking Iboga, I was having full-on conversations with the brother who had died before I was born, and interacting with various ancestors and spirits I had never seen in my sober life.

Taking Iboga opened my eyes to the existence of other realms. It also taught me that there are *many* ways to receive information. When I was on Iboga, I could see exactly which wild herbs I was supposed to gather to help my mother's cancer—not only which plants, but exactly where they grew. When the Iboga journey was over, I went to the places I had seen in my vision and, sure enough, those exact plants were right where they were supposed to be. I gathered the plants and prepared them in the way I had seen, and they helped my mother heal from her cancer.

When I went back to high school after taking Iboga for the first time, I realized I had changed. I had become very sensitive. I could discern the real meaning behind people's words in a way I hadn't been able to before. I could tell what people were really thinking and feeling, despite the masks they wore on the outside. It was as if I was suddenly privy to streams of information that had been invisible to me before. All of my friends seemed to be living in a small, limited world, while I had just experienced a much vaster one. How could I shrink myself back down to fit in the old world again?

At that age, there was no way I was going to tell my friends what I was going through. I could hardly sit down at the lunch table and say, "Hey guys, I just traveled to a magical realm where spirits told me to go behind the train tracks and pick some wild plants!" Instead, I stuffed it down and pretended it wasn't happening. I did my best to ignore my newfound awareness, and channeled my energy into acting normal in front of my peers. I pretended *not* to know what people were thinking and feeling, and *not* to have other insights that were coming into my head all the time. Most importantly, I buried myself in books, taking on the persona of a serious student to avoid the social interactions that had become so painful and confusing to me. I denied my real self, and created a self that was more acceptable to those around me.

Still, aspects of my real self leaked through from time to time, and when that happened, it was devastating. "There goes Marie, getting all spooky again," people would say. At that time, Cameroon was modernizing rapidly. Even though the adults had asked me to do Iboga, they simultaneously expected me to carry on as a normal modern girl—quite the double bind.

Decades later, I was working as an anesthesiologist in California when I had a sort of awakening—or, more accurately, a reawakening. I began to see people's thoughts and emotions and even catch glimpses of their family histories, just as I had when I was a teenager. When a patient would come into my room, my brain would start to download all this information about them whether I wanted to or not. It was overwhelming, and I wasn't sure where to go with it.

Although I was working in a hospital where everything was all science, all the time, I found myself creating a sacred space in my anesthesia room. I meditated on my anesthesia machine. I kept crystals and essential oils in my desk. I was very attuned to my patients' energy, and often knew things about them I had no rational way of knowing—their grandparents' names and professions, for example. The surgeons at the hospital began to ask me to be their patients' anesthesiologist more and more frequently, because I was so good at calming the patients down. I knew that my "secret sauce" was energy work—but nobody at the hospital wanted to hear about that.

I didn't want my colleagues to see me as a New Age kook—after all, I'd gone to medical school, just like them, and I believed in science as much as ever.

But, just like when I was fourteen years old, I found myself putting more and more energy into denial—suppressing my gifts, and pretending to be something I wasn't. Although I had a sense that I was meant to be an energy healer (as much as if not more than I was meant to be a traditional doctor), I struggled with how and when to let this aspect of my identity come out. In the meantime, I experienced a profound sense of depression, alienation, and despair.

I realized that I was living with a denial wound. At fourteen, I'd had to hide my gifts in order to gain acceptance from my family and peers, even if those people were benefiting from the very same gifts they required me to hide. Now, the same thing was happening all over again. As an adult, however, I had the opportunity to stop living in denial, and walk into the world as my true self. I decided to stop practicing anesthesiology and become a full-time shaman and energy worker, before any more years of my life were given over to the service of an identity that wasn't really *me*.

Origins of the Denial Wound

The denial wound drains your energy. It saps your chi. It causes you to feel that you are living a lie. And although it can manifest at any time in a person's life, it usually has its origins in childhood.

Some children are encouraged to express their true selves loudly and clearly—to voice their opinions and preferences, their passions and desires. But many of us are not so lucky. Instead, we are taught from a young age that our real selves are unacceptable, and we should only express those aspects of ourselves that make our parents happy. This strategy may work for a while, but over the years it can lead to depression, burnout, and a lingering sense that something is wrong.

Here are some common ways the denial wound comes into being:

- Being forced to hide a key aspect of your identity

- Witnessing another person being shamed for a characteristic you share

- Having parents who insist upon a high level of compliance and conformity

- Having parents who themselves are denying a key aspect of their identities

- Being punished for expressing difference

- Being punished for expressing your true emotions and opinions

- Being raised by parents who value achievement over self-fulfillment

Although we all wear masks from time to time, those of us with denial wounds become prisoners of our masks, unable to let our true faces show at any time, in any context, even with our closest friends— sometimes even when we're alone. In that sense, the denial wound robs you of the opportunity to be truly known.

Signs You Are Living with a Denial Wound

The denial wound can manifest as suppressing your true identity, vocation, or path, but it can also show up as routine, everyday denials of your true feelings, opinions, and preferences. A client of mine had been in an unhappy relationship for almost ten years. She had recently separated from her husband and filed for divorce, but she was still running a business with him and spending nearly all of her time with him. Even as she took steps to get divorced, she was still in denial about the marriage being over. She was so used to suppressing her feelings that it was hard for her to make the changes that she knew she wanted.

If you have a hard time knowing what you really want or expressing who you really are, chances are you're living with a denial wound. Here are some other telltale signs:

- You feel that nobody knows the real you.

- You feel that you have to wear a mask to please others.

- You feel a sense of falseness about your life.

- You frequently daydream about a life radically different from the one you are living.

- You feel exhausted by the demands of putting up a facade.

- You have few or no close friends.

- You feel a sense of resentment toward people who are embodying the identity you can't permit for yourself.

- You are afraid of being caught or found out.

- You refrain from sharing your true opinions and preferences.

- You chronically hide aspects of yourself—for example, hiding your books where nobody can see them, or keeping your hobbies a secret.

- You feel jealous of others who seem more free than you could ever be.

- You feel burdened by the passage of time and have begun to accumulate regrets.

Even though the denial wound is quieter than some of the other wounds, its effects can be devastating. Like a slow leak, it can keep you in a constant state of low-level depletion, never quite living up to your full potential or enjoying the many pleasures that life has to offer. Although you may tell yourself that you're content to just live with it, the denial wound is just as urgent as the louder, flashier wounds, and just as deserving of attention.

Here are some of the most common ways the denial wound shows up.

Holding on to Regret

When you bury your heart's desire, regret is inevitable—especially as you grow older and realize that this lifetime is your one chance to live your dream. Not only that, but nobody else is going to come along and make that dream happen for you—you have to take those risks for yourself. This sense of regret may be quiet at first; but as the years pass, and you watch other people pursuing their dreams while you remain trapped in a false identity, living the life that your parents, spouse, or religious leaders have defined for you, you might find this feeling growing more insistent and painful.

A client of mine had followed in her parents' footsteps and gone to law school. She was making a high income as a corporate attorney, but was dogged by the sense that she was living a lie. As soon as she left her house in the morning, it seemed that she had to put on a mask, becoming the competent professional everyone wanted and needed her to be. Not only that, but she had to play nice with her clients—wealthy CEOs whose politics often clashed with her own. Her entire job consisted of helping rich, powerful men get even richer, and looking happy about it, too.

Ten years into this career, she already felt like her life was passing her by. She wondered what her life would have been like if she'd followed her passion, which was writing, instead of going to law school. She had developed chronic insomnia and felt a physical sense of dread about walking out her front door in the morning. Sometimes, she locked herself in the bathroom at work and cried. It felt like her whole body was rebelling against the work she had to do. Yet in her headshot on the firm's website, she looked serene and confident, the perfect, high-achieving lawyer.

This client's parents had gotten divorced when she was six, and her mother soon remarried a man who was bland, boring, and sometimes bad-tempered. My client did not like her new stepfather at all, but when her mother told her to smile for the wedding photographs, she did as she was told. At that age, she had already learned that the family's image was everything. Her own emotions took a distant second place compared to the importance of projecting happiness and togetherness to the outside world.

Now, that ability to deny her emotions had led her into a life in which she was truly unhappy. As long as she could smile for things and people she detested, she despaired of ever having a life worth smiling for. "I can make everyone happy except myself," she told me. "It's my superpower. But what will I feel at the end of my life, when I haven't done a single thing that *I* wanted to do?"

Feeling Highly Anxious

The denial wound protects its own existence by flooding the mind with anxiety. *I can't come out of the closet—what will my ex-girlfriend think? . . . If I leave my high-paying job, how will I survive?* Instead of looking at how much it's costing you to live in denial, you worry about what would happen if you ever showed up as your authentic self. These anxious thoughts make it seem relatively appealing to continue living from a place of denial even if you are feeling sick, drained, and exhausted as a result of it.

A client of mine had a denial wound from being gay and in the closet. When he was a small boy, he had overheard his grandparents whispering about "those disgusting homosexuals," and that incident had flooded him with shame and fear. At that age, he already knew that he had no interest in girls—but after hearing his grandparents talking, he made a point of chasing girls around the playground, and mimicking the early attempts at flirtation that he observed in other boys.

By the time he was in high school, his denial of his sexuality was complete. He had a serious girlfriend, and he even made nasty comments about the gay kids at school, in an effort to distance himself from them. He only engaged in "masculine" activities like football and video games, and made sure that his body language conveyed only masculinity at all times. At the same time, he developed chronic depression and anxiety. Although he couldn't articulate it to himself, he lived in fear of his gay side slipping out. The effort of constant vigilance left him feeling drained and exhausted.

At the time this client came to see me, his grandparents had just died. With their passing, he wondered if he was finally safe to express his true sexuality. As an adult, he could see that homosexuality was gaining wider acceptance—and that, while the occasional experience of disapproval or rudeness was unpleasant, it would no longer be as devastating as it was when he was a child. But at the same time, his mind continued to pump out anxiety whenever he considered it. What would his brother think? His old friends? The gay kids he'd bullied in high school?

Instead of focusing on the potential benefits of coming out, he was tunnel-visioned on the potential costs. His denial wound was desperately fighting for its own continued existence by convincing him that it would *never* be safe to step into the world as his true self.

Feeling Resentful

When you are living with a denial wound, you may feel intense resentment when you encounter a person who is living your own buried dream. Instead of accepting and grieving whatever it is that you have lost, you may project your anger onto others, blaming and judging them for their choices.

If you feel intense resentment toward or irritation around a certain type of person, chances are that person has given him- or herself permission to do or be something that you would desperately like to do or be yourself. So much of life consists of permission— first of all, the permission given or withheld by the adults in your life when you are a child, and secondly, the permission you give or withhold from yourself.

A client of mine couldn't stand to see happy couples with babies, having decided to forgo children herself as a statement about sustainability and climate change. She'd spent her twenties as an environmental activist, and had even published numerous articles speaking out against overpopulation. As she entered her thirties, she suddenly found herself wanting children after all. She decided to suppress this desire, rather than acknowledge it and risk coming across as a hypocrite. At the same time, her judgment of people who *did* have babies became harsher and more outspoken than ever.

Her friendships suffered, as her friends rightly perceived that she was not a safe person to talk to about their own true feelings about reproduction and a variety of other subjects. By denying her own feelings, she created a kind of force field of denial in which nobody else could express his or her true self either.

Risks of the Denial Wound

Left untreated, the denial wound has a high likelihood of being passed on to future generations. A mother who never had the chance to express her true self will unconsciously discourage her children from living their own truth. A father who had to hide who he really was may nudge his own children into similar behavior, even if he intends to do the opposite. I know that my own denial wound was highly influenced by my mother, my grandmother, and all the women before them who had to conform to the expectations of a patriarchal society.

The denial wound challenges us to be courageous. Although you may have brokered a truce with this wound, agreeing to live a diminished version of the life you really want, or express only a fraction of your true self, the costs of this truce are greater than you might realize—and the benefits of healing this wound are more wonderful than you can imagine.

The good news is, the denial wound can end with you. By working with the healing practices in the next chapter, you can resolve this wound for yourself and future generations.

Part 3

Healing Practices

The denial wound is my favorite wound to work with, because the transformation I see in my clients is so joyous and can often be quite swift. Time after time, I've watched even my most fearful clients give themselves permission to live as their authentic selves, and make the changes that will allow them to live without regret. By working with a handful of simple practices, you can develop the courage required to shed the old rules you've been living by, and establish a healthier relationship with life.

When I was a kid, I learned that the quickest way to get approval from the adults in my life was to read. Whenever adults saw me reading, they'd say, "Oh, Marie's such a good student. She's always studying, always carrying a book around." While it was true that I enjoyed reading, I often used the excuse of studying to avoid interacting with people—especially after my experience with Iboga. Although I would have liked to express my newfound sensitivity and awareness in many different ways—by painting, for example, or singing—I knew that doing these things would only call negative attention to me.

Decades later, when I was struggling to decide how much to reveal my spiritual side at work, or whether I should even reveal it at all, a friend of mine invited me to participate in a painting challenge on social media. "I can't paint," I told her. "And even if I was going to paint something, how can I possibly post it online where people can see?"

"Just give it a try," said my friend. "You'll be surprised."

I didn't want to let her down, so, despite my trepidation, I bought a few cheap canvases and some paint, and began to play around. Before I knew it, I'd produced several bold, striking paintings—and when I posted photos of them online, I immediately got offers from people wanting to buy them. It turns out I *do* have artistic talent—plenty of it! I wondered if leaning into my artistic side could help me in my transition from medical doctor to shaman.

I began to work with my denial wound by intentionally engaging in creative practice—painting, singing, dancing, drumming. I realized nobody was going to live my life for me, so if I was going to make the transition I needed, I had to get over my fears and get on with it. The result was that I became much happier. The subtle resentment I had toward so-called creative people drained away, because I had given myself permission to inhabit my own creativity. I also felt a delicious expansion of possibilities for my life. My anxiety about "coming out" as spiritual began to diminish, and I started taking concrete steps to establish my new life as a shaman.

However, when I finally told a colleague of mine about my spiritual path, she laughed out loud. "Oh, Marie," she said, "we all *knew* you were spiritual. Did you really think you were hiding it all that time?" Like so many people with denial wounds, the person I was really hiding from was myself.

Healing Practice: Exploring Courageous Self-Inquiry

If the thought of expressing your true self in public terrifies you, you can start by expressing yourself in the safety and privacy of your journal. If you are living with a deep denial wound, chances are you've never let yourself articulate your true opinions, wishes, and preferences—even to yourself! This practice will give you the opportunity to do exactly that.

Grab your notebook and complete the following prompts with complete honesty—no holds barred. Don't worry if you have to beat around the bush a little before coming to your answer. Take as long as you need. Remember, you can destroy these pages right away if you choose. Nobody is going to see them except you.

- If I took off my mask, people would see . . .

- I've never told anyone how I really feel about . . .

- If I wasn't afraid of what people would think, I would . . .

- If I wasn't worried about my family's reaction, I would . . .

- My ideal life would look like . . .

- My ideal romantic arrangement would look like . . .

- If I knew I couldn't fail, I would . . .

Here's what I wrote down when I did this exercise:

If I took off my mask, people would see . . . a shaman who perceives energy fields, hears the voices of the ancestors, and can see the five wounds of the heart.

I've never told anyone how I really feel about... my mother! She did so much to hurt me and my sister when we were young, and it took me a long time to get in touch with my own pain about what she did.

If I wasn't afraid of what people would think, I would ... walk down the street with my drum, inviting strangers to join me in a spontaneous celebration of being alive.

If I wasn't worried about my family's reaction, I would ... tell the truth about my experiences with Iboga.

My ideal life would look like ... sharing a message of joy and healing with all of humanity.

My ideal romantic arrangement would look like ... two or three lovers in different cities around the world, whom I could visit at my leisure.

If I knew I couldn't fail, I would ... go live in the Amazon and open my own retreat center.

By allowing yourself to write down your real answers to these questions, you are practicing authenticity in a safe container, and giving yourself the beginnings of permission to live these truths. The more time you spend writing about who you really are and what you really want, the more normal it will feel to express your true self in other contexts— for example, with friends and coworkers. Eventually, you may look back and wonder how you ever found it so hard to express these things.

Healing Practice: Writing a Denial Letter

When you think about your parents, your church, your schoolteachers, or the other people who helped install your denial wound, chances are you feel some anger. Rather than stewing in anger and regret, it can be helpful to imagine the person in question sending you an apology letter. This healing practice can give you a sense of closure while expanding your compassion for the person who hurt you.

A client of mine had been shamed by a teacher for her "poor" and "sloppy" artwork in elementary school. These comments inhibited her natural exuberance, and made her think she was terrible at art—never mind the fact that *all* children are fabulous artists. This is the letter she imagined her teacher writing to her:

Dear Solange,

I'm so sorry I made those comments about your painting when you were my second-grade student. In the intervening years, I have heard from many of my former students about how my discouraging words affected them. I realize that I inadvertently projected my own fears and anxieties onto all of you, and for that I am deeply sorry.

The truth is, I always wanted to be an artist myself, but I was forced to take a more practical path in order to earn income for my family. I was never allowed to do "frivolous" things like paint or draw, but always had to be the good, responsible daughter and get a good job. Whenever I saw children like you entertaining dreams of being artists, I wanted to squash those dreams because I was never allowed to follow them myself. I wish I could go back and give you the encouragement you needed, instead of shutting you down.

I hope someday you follow your artistic leanings with joy, no matter what I or anyone else said to discourage you when you were younger. It would make me happy to know that you are painting now, as an adult, because you do have talent, and have had it all along.

Sincerely,

Mrs. Smith

When you take the time to write yourself a letter from the perspective of a person who has hurt you, you are using the power of your imagination to give yourself the healing you need—no outside participation required. By creating your own sense of closure, you also reduce the likelihood that you will pass this wound on to your own children, or to other people in your life.

Healing Practice: Writing Positive Affirmations

What kind of messages are you feeding your own mind and soul? If you are living with a denial wound, chances are those messages are colored by fear: *I shouldn't, I'm not good enough, It won't work out, They'll think I'm crazy.* The denial wound thrives on fear—fear of failure, fear of rejection, fear of a hundred different anxiety-provoking scenarios. When you replace your fearful thoughts with confident, loving ones, the denial wound naturally begins to shrink, until one day you wake up to realize you haven't heard from it at all in months or years.

I asked a client of mine to write down her most common thoughts about herself. Here's what she wrote:

I can't.

I shouldn't.

I'm so ugly/sloppy/lazy/stupid.

I bet they hate me.

Why aren't I getting this?

If I would just try harder . . .

There I go, screwing it up again . . .

Next, I asked her to write down a second list, this time of positive statements about herself:

I am beautiful.

I am talented.

I've got this.

I can do this.

People like me.

I like myself.

Everything's OK.

This is fun.

I'm getting better at this every day.

Every time her brain fed her a statement from the first list, I asked her to consciously repeat a statement from the second list. Not only that, but we decided she would repeat a statement from the second list whenever she remembered to do so, whether or not it had been preceded by a negative statement.

Over the next few weeks, something marvelous happened. The positive affirmations saturated her mind with messages of confidence, love, and unconditional acceptance. By repeating these affirmations day after day, her outlook on life began to change. I could see a noticeable difference in her posture and body language. The more she came to genuinely like herself, the easier it became for her to express her true self to other people—a truly virtuous cycle.

Healing Practice: Risking Exposure

If you are living with a denial wound, you may find it very difficult to take risks—for example, making a disclosure to a friend, speaking up in public, trying a new activity you might not be good at right away, even seemingly simple things like wearing the clothes you really like, or playing your favorite music in a context where someone else might overhear it. Maybe it feels safe to keep a very neutral exterior, and keep your wild side locked up where nobody can see it. But if you never take those risks, you'll miss out on all the joy and connection that becomes available when you show up in the world as your true self.

You can test the waters by taking small risks—disclosing parts of your true self to other people, and gaining confidence that you can tolerate their reactions. For example, you might try some of these things:

- Tell a friend, neighbor, or coworker about the last book you read or movie you really loved, even if you're afraid they'll judge you for your taste.

- Drive down the street with your favorite music playing and the windows rolled down.

- Wear a piece of clothing or jewelry that says something about you—and be ready with a story if people ask about it.

- Tell a friend about the last crazy dream you had.

- The next time you're faced with a group decision, state your real preference without waiting to see what everyone else says first.

- Post a photo or video on social media of yourself doing something you really love, even if you're not an expert at it.

- Take a class, workshop, or lesson in a subject that interests you, with the intention of learning and having fun.

- Go to a support group in which people share difficult experiences, and tell a story from your own life.

- Talk to a stranger at a café, or on the bus. Give them a genuine compliment, or ask a question, and let yourself be surprised by the response.

- Take a trip to a town where you don't know anyone. Go as your true self, whatever that means to you. Where does your true self go for dinner? What does she do in the evening? What does she wear? Who does she talk to? Give yourself permission to do those things.

It's never too late to start dissolving old bonds and let your real self emerge. By practicing taking risks, you will gradually realize that the world doesn't fall apart when you show up as yourself—in fact, you may discover you have *more* friends, *more* opportunities, and *more* to live for than you did when you were living in denial.

Signs Your Denial Wound Is Healing

When I was living with an unhealed denial wound, I often felt anxious, depressed, and drained. I couldn't enjoy life, because so much of my energy was going into hiding who I really was. I also found it hard to make close connections with other people, because I was very guarded and afraid of showing anyone my real self. When I began to heal this wound by embarking on my path as an energy healer, I felt a tremendous amount of joy permeating my day-to-day life. I smiled so much that people would tease me about it—"Oh Marie, you're so happy all the time. I'll have what you're having!" I also made some of the closest friends I've ever had, people who shared an interest in shamanism and heart-opening work. None of this would have been possible if I'd stayed hidden behind my safe identity as a medical doctor.

When you heal a denial wound, you free up so much energy that was otherwise going into hiding and suppressing your true nature. This energy can give you a new lease on life—you might start a new career or relationship, undergo a radical physical transformation, or simply radiate love and acceptance where before you were radiating anxiety and fear.

Your denial wound is healing if you notice any of the following things:

- An increase in happiness and ease
- A reduction in anxiety and depression
- Greater ease in making friends and romantic connections
- More laughter
- Better conversations
- Open, unguarded posture
- A reduction in somatic symptoms such as headaches and fevers
- A sense of hopefulness about life
- A newfound ability to see possibilities and opportunities
- Greater self-love

Hidden Treasure: Authenticity

It should come as no surprise that the hidden treasure buried at the bottom of the denial wound is authenticity. Although we associate authenticity with being real or genuine, the English word *authentic* comes from the ancient Greek *authentikos*, meaning "acting on one's own authority." In other words, to be authentic means to seek your *own* permission to act, do, and be, rather than waiting for some outside authority to tell you it's OK. The truth is, *you* are the only one who can give yourself permission to live the life you want—nobody else can do that for you, no matter how encouraging they may be.

When you are authentically yourself, the painful gap between your real self and the self you show to the world disappears. You no longer have to curate a self for every new person you meet, because you're always there—whole, complete, vibrant, and alive. Even though people may occasionally respond to you with dislike or judgment, you realize that you can handle this calmly and with good humor. Living with a mask is a constant drain, while running into the occasional experience of dislike or disapproval is no more than an intermittent discomfort.

When you live as your authentic self, you can die with no regrets, because you know that you didn't bury or suppress something that was important to you. You also become more wonderful to be around, because people sense that they don't have to suppress *their* true selves around *you*. Instead, your presence gives other people a sense of joy and freedom, because they can instinctively feel that it's safe to let loose around you. In this sense, your authenticity is a gift to the whole community.

Part 4

The Judgment Wound

I will never forget the day I went to church with my mother and her new husband, the first time she brought him home to Cameroon. At that time, divorce was extremely rare in Cameroon, and even rarer within our tight-knit Catholic community. I had had early inklings that divorce was considered shameful when a close school friend of mine began to introduce me as her "cousin" instead of her friend, to avoid having to explain who my parents were and why they didn't live together, and from the whispers of certain adults who looked down on my mother's decision.

Still, as a child, I was unaware of just how much stigma divorce carried until that particular Sunday. When my mother stood up to receive communion, there was an audible gasp throughout the church. My grandmother and our neighbors gave my mother a sharp look, and she sat back down. Divorced people were not allowed to receive communion—that's how big of a sin it was in the Catholic Church.

Even though the congregation's judgment was directed at my mother rather than me, I felt profoundly shamed. My school friend's odd behavior came into sharper focus, as did the increased scrutiny I'd been experiencing from my teachers and other adults. I suddenly understood that my family situation was "wrong," and that, by extension, I was suspect.

After that moment in church, I became very sensitive to other people's judgments—and I began to make more of my own, in retaliation. If I sensed that another girl was judging me for my family situation, I'd think, *Well, you're fat and ugly, and you'll never be as smart as I am.* I studied hard to make sure I was always at the top of my class and therefore "better" than everyone else. If I made even one little mistake on my homework assignments, I would judge myself harshly, castigating myself for being stupid and careless.

When I got into medical school—one of only four women in my class—the pressure from the outside and the inside mounted. It felt like everyone around me was waiting for me to fail. I couldn't show any weakness whatsoever, or my teachers and classmates would use it as proof that women did not belong in medicine. I learned to judge myself just as harshly as they judged me, and to hold myself to impossibly high standards at all times. I forgot that these judgmental voices had come from the *outside*, and I started to feel like they were mine.

By the time I was a full-fledged adult, I had become a full-fledged perfectionist, too. I double- and triple-checked all my work, making sure that nobody could ever catch me making a mistake. I avoided taking risks or engaging in activities in which I was not 100 percent confident I would be successful. If I made even the tiniest slipup—forgetting to return a phone call promptly, or getting a parking ticket—I felt so much guilt and shame I was practically suicidal.

It was hard for me to have close friends, because I suspected that everyone was waiting to find fault with me, and there was no way I was going to let that happen. At the same time, I was constantly seeking out the flaws in other people, as a way of reassuring myself that at least I wasn't as bad as *them*. This way of life left me isolated and unhappy. I had the career I'd always dreamed of, but I was trapped in a state of hypervigilance, unable to let my hair down and *just be average* for a while.

Origins of the Judgment Wound

When we are children, our natural state is joy and ease. It doesn't occur to us that we are anything less than perfect exactly the way we are. If we are lucky, our parents validate this innate perfection, while guiding us toward appropriate behavior. If we do something disruptive, for example, our parents would ask us to behave differently, without implying that we are innately bad, wrong, or guilty.

The judgment wound occurs when an important person in our life shames us for who we are, instead of merely correcting our mistakes in a loving way. For example, a client of mine had a painful memory of attending a birthday party as a child. When she helped herself to a second piece of cake without asking, her mother took her aside and scolded her angrily, saying, "That's not only rude, it's disgusting. A girl like you doesn't need to eat two pieces of cake."

When she heard her mother's words, my client understood that not only was eating two pieces of cake disgusting, but *she* was disgusting. In that moment, the sense of safety she'd felt in her relationship with her mother was irrevocably damaged. She saw that her mother's love was not, in fact, unconditional, but depended on her behaving in a certain way. Her fear of being shamed again lead her to scrupulously avoid any more "disgusting" behaviors, particularly when it came to food—which ultimately left her with an eating disorder.

Here are some experiences that could cause a judgment wound:

- Growing up with highly critical parents

- Feeling that your parents' or caregivers' love depended on you meeting certain criteria of behavior and self-presentation

- Being shamed by an important adult in your life for something you said or did

- Being shamed by an important institution in your life—for example, your school or church

- Being neglected, which children experience as a source of shame

- Being required to meet impossible standards by your family, school, or church

- Having parents who expressed frequent disappointment with you

- Having parents who were highly judgmental of each other or of themselves

As children, we are natural mimics. When we witness the adults in our lives being critical and judgmental, we internalize these behaviors and turn them against ourselves, until we start to feel like constant judgment and criticism are a natural state of being, instead of the damaging aberrations they really are.

Signs You Are Living with a Judgment Wound

The judgment wound is characterized by perfectionism. When we fear judgment, our only option is to be perfect—so we do whatever we can to be above reproach, even if that means blaming others, making excuses, or telling lies. We find it difficult or impossible to admit weakness or wrongdoing, even to our closest friends and family members, and this makes it difficult to get close to anyone. We drown ourselves in work, exercise, and self-improvement, hoping we can eliminate the last traces of imperfection from our lives.

Meanwhile, our self-esteem suffers. The harder we try to live up to impossible standards, the more mediocre we feel inside. At its most extreme, the judgment wound can lead to self-hatred—a complete rejection of the self, which can be accompanied by eating disorders, self-harm, or even suicide. Knowing we can never be perfect, we may give in to anger and despair, lashing out at ourselves or others, and completely losing touch with the innate beauty and complexity of life.

The judgment wound places a filter on your experience of reality, making it seem like something terrible will happen if you let anyone see the side of you that is disorganized, sloppy, overwhelmed, confused, or not completely on the ball. This can lead to substance abuse, unsafe sex or affairs, or other ways of blowing off steam as a result of living under unbearable pressure.

Here are some telltale signs that you are living with a judgment wound:

- You are a perfectionist.

- You have higher expectations for yourself than you do for others.

- You constantly find fault with yourself and others.

- You have a lot of "shoulds."

- You have a lot of "if only's."

- You rake yourself over the coals for past mistakes.

- You don't like to be seen when you're not looking your best.

- You overexercise.

- You have a punitive relationship with food and may be prone to eating disorders.

- You feel an outsize sense of shame when you make ordinary mistakes.

- Your relationships with friends, coworkers, and romantic partners are characterized by anxiety.

- You are irritable.

- You are constantly comparing yourself to other people.

- You find it difficult to take pride in your accomplishments.

- You always feel you're at risk of falling behind, no matter how much effort you put in.

The judgment wound is most apparent in our inner dialogue—the voices in our heads reflecting on everything we say and do. If you have a deep judgment wound, these voices might be utterly toxic, nagging and criticizing you throughout the day: *You're so stupid. How could you even think that would work? Look at you, pigging out again!* No matter how much you scramble to appease these voices—by trying harder, worrying more, or exerting more willpower—they always find new ways you're failing or humiliating yourself.

Let's take a look at some common ways the judgment wound shows up.

Being Self-Critical

A friend of mine was such a perfectionist that she couldn't make even minor mistakes without raking herself over the coals for days or even weeks. She expected herself to be perfectly efficient at all times, running her life like the proverbial well-oiled machine, never accounting for the fact that human beings were not designed to be 100 percent efficient. When she was a few minutes late to an appointment, or forgot her library books at home and had to return them on a separate trip, her self-criticism was so intense you'd think she'd screwed up a critical military operation, resulting in thousands of deaths.

At work, she shocked colleagues by apologizing profusely for making a typo on a PowerPoint presentation. In her mind, this mistake was unbearably shameful. She was certain her coworkers were furious with her, that she was about to be demoted or fired, and that her entire career was over. Even when coworkers assured her that it was no big deal, she couldn't shake a sense of doom—as if she had come close to jeopardizing her very survival.

Her father had been an Army general who punished his children severely for making their beds incorrectly and other minor mistakes. As a child, she had learned that the best way to avoid trouble was to punish *herself* before anyone else had a chance to find fault with her. Her fear of disapproval was so great that she was constantly on the verge of tears, even though she was as honest, dutiful, and well-behaved as a child can be. This pattern had carried on into her adult life, with the result that she always felt herself to be right on the edge of screwing everything up and bringing on disaster.

When you are living with a judgment wound, nothing you do ever seems quite good enough. You are primed to see the ways that you are failing, falling behind, and screwing up, while ignoring all the ways you're succeeding. Even when you do manage to check all the boxes, you still can't relax, because the possibility of failure is always right around the corner. You judge yourself constantly, while refusing to appreciate yourself for your good qualities or for the many tasks you accomplish each day.

Frequently Finding Fault with Others and the World

Not only does the judgment wound cause you to criticize yourself, it causes you to cast a judgmental eye on other people and on life in general. *This town was so pretty before they built those ugly modern condos*, you might think, or *My neighbors should really stop their kids from playing games on their tablets all the time.* Constant fault-finding can come to seem normal—just an intelligent person's reaction to a world that is frustratingly imperfect. But believe it or not, fault-finding is how the judgment wound perpetuates itself, preventing you from ever feeling real peace.

A client of mine was an engineer. He couldn't open a door, drink a mug of coffee, or press a button on a TV remote without finding nine or ten problems with how those objects had been designed. He was the same way in his relationships: he was forever complaining about how his coworkers needed to change their attitudes, his wife needed to stop reading those useless self-help books, and his parents needed to get organized and stop living their lives in such a scatterbrained, haphazard way. During our sessions, he even complained about my French-Cameroonian accent, and the way I ran my business!

He told himself that he had no choice but to suffer in this poorly designed world, surrounded by stubborn people who wouldn't run their lives the way he thought they should. In truth, his suffering was the result of a judgment wound. As a child, he'd had ADHD, which wasn't diagnosed until decades later. His parents and teachers were always criticizing him for behaving in ways they didn't understand. *If you would only pay attention*, they would say, or *If you would only do your homework at a reasonable time, instead of leaving it to the last minute.* They were forever finding fault with him, for reasons entirely outside of his control.

Rather than feeling the pain of these unfair demands, he learned to copy his parents and teachers by finding fault in everything. As long as he was finding fault with the world, he could distract himself from his own shameful imperfection. In truth, the criticisms he lobbed at the things and people around him were projections of his own self-loathing—symptoms of his judgment wound. By joining his parents and teachers in criticizing everything, he could also gain some small degree of acceptance by proving he was "just like them."

Lying

If you are terrified of making mistakes or being seen as less than perfect, you may be in the habit of lying or even cheating to cover up your ordinary weaknesses. Even though you may not be inherently manipulative or deceitful, you could find yourself telling a surprising number of lies to avoid the shame you fear would be forthcoming if people found out just how flawed and average you were.

For example, a client of mine was a very honest and sincere person in most ways, but when she accidentally backed her car into a fire hydrant, damaging the rear bumper, she automatically lied to her friends, husband, and coworkers about what had happened. Even though it was a minor and completely normal mistake, of the type that most adults will someday make if they drive a car for long enough, she was so afraid of being seen as careless or irresponsible that she couldn't confess to what had happened.

Another client of mine was a tenured professor at a prestigious university. When her research results didn't come out as she'd hoped, she fudged the numbers to get the results (and the news headlines) she wanted. Although she knew that it would be terrible for her reputation if she got caught, the fear of being seen as "average" was just too strong. She lied to avoid the shame she imagined she would feel if her community found out that her experiment had not gone as planned, but in the process she took on the *real* shame of deceiving her students and colleagues.

On a subconscious level, each of these women was afraid that if her friends, partner, or colleagues found out she had "failed," they would stop loving her. Although neither of them was aware of this, they each believed that love was conditional on being perfect—and with stakes like that, who wouldn't lie?

Risks of the Judgment Wound

Left untreated, the judgment wound can wreak havoc on your life, keeping you in a constant state of fear and stress, and robbing you of the natural joy of being alive. Not only does the judgment wound prevent you from enjoying your own accomplishments, but it diminishes your ability to enjoy the many gifts that other people share with you on a daily basis. If you can only see the flaws in other people, and are constantly subjecting your friends and loved ones to a filter through which you can only see the ways they're letting you down, your relationships will suffer. As long as you consider yourself to be either superior or inferior to others, you cannot look into their eyes and say, *namaste*—the light in me sees and acknowledges the light in you.

The good news is, once you become aware of this wound, you can begin to release it, giving yourself the unconditional love that was your birthright all along—and freeing up your ability to offer that same love and gratitude to others. In the next chapter, I will share my favorite tools for doing exactly that.

Part 4

Healing Practices

By the time I became an adult, my judgment wound was so firmly established that judging myself and others felt normal to me. Because I was constantly looking out for the ways that other people were judging me, I was always on the defensive; at the same time, I was quick to condemn others, with little curiosity about their reasons for behaving the way they did, and even less compassion.

When I came to the United States for my medical residency, a fellow resident invited me to a party at her family's home. I was excited to be in the US—a long-held dream of mine—and eager to prove myself to my new colleagues. But when this fellow resident introduced me to her parents, and told them I was from Cameroon, they looked at me like an animal in a zoo. "You're from Africa?" they said. "*Wowwwww.* How did you learn to speak English? That's just incredible that you grew up there, and now you're here."

Looking back, I can see that they weren't trying to be rude or patronizing. They were ignorant, and in their ignorance, genuinely in awe that a person from Africa—which, in their imagination, was a war-torn wasteland where people dressed in skins, lived in huts, and jabbered at each other in a "primitive" language—could learn English, make her way to America, and become a medical specialist.

But at the time, my judgment wound flared right up. "You know, it *is* amazing," I said sarcastically. "Last week, I was fighting over a banana with a wild monkey, and now here I am!"

I stormed away, thinking about how rude, stupid, and racist they were. It didn't occur to me to be curious about the conditions of their lives. It was only much later that I found out that my colleague's parents were factory workers with only a high school education. Whereas I'd grown up with chauffeurs and gone to an international school in the capital of Cameroon, they had spent their entire lives in the same poor, rural county of the United States, with little exposure to other cultures besides what they'd seen on TV.

When I learned these facts about my colleagues' parents, I felt bad for my angry response. I realized my judgment wound was blocking my heart and preventing me from feeling compassion for other people. Not only that, but the endless stream of judgments that filled my mind was like a toxic cloud of smoke, keeping my entire being in a state of negativity and ill health. I decided it was time to heal my judgment wound, and recover my ability to be curious and compassionate about myself and others.

It can feel scary to step outside of judgment. We fear that if we stop judging and criticizing ourselves, we will become self-indulgent or lazy, or we will make terrible mistakes and humiliate ourselves. And we fear that if we stop judging and criticizing others, they will run over us rough-shod, getting away with bad behavior. We believe it is our criticism that keeps us safe, when in fact this criticism is preventing us from reaching our full potential and enjoying the richness of life.

When I started to work with my judgment wound, a funny thing happened—at least, funny in hindsight. Every time I noticed myself having a judgmental thought, I would immediately criticize myself for having it. In other words, I would judge myself for being too judgmental! It took some practice to allow those judgmental thoughts to arise, and simply notice them with curiosity and good humor, instead of taking them as an opportunity to carry on with my old patterns. As you heal your judgment wound, remember not to judge yourself for continuing to have judgments—over time, they will naturally fade away.

Healing Practice: Acknowledging the Positive

When you are living with a judgment wound, you develop tunnel vision. You can only see the negative—the ways you are failing, falling short, or getting left behind. Healing from the judgment wound involves replacing this negative filter with a positive one. Although it takes conscious effort at first and may feel awkward, you can train yourself to see and acknowledge the positive in yourself and your life—not just once a day, but moment to moment. You can begin this training by intentionally calling up memories of times when you succeeded, accomplished something meaningful, or did kind things for others. Answer the following prompts in your journal:

- What character traits are you most proud to possess?

- Which accomplishments are you most proud of?

- In what ways are you a wonderful friend, coworker, partner, or family member?

- Think of a time when you did something kind or generous for another person, and write about it.

- Think of a time when you persevered to solve a problem, and write about it.

A client of mine had been mired in depression for the better part of a decade, hostage to his relentless inner critic. Answering these prompts was the first time in *years* he had formed a positive thought about himself. Here's what he wrote:

What character traits are you most proud to possess? I am honest and fair, even in situations in which it would be easy for me to take advantage of others. I genuinely care about other people, and always do my best to make their lives better.

Which accomplishments are you most proud of? I learned to play violin as an adult. This took so much commitment, dedication, and humility! Most adults who try to learn instruments don't get very far, but I persevered, and now people assume I must have learned as a child.

In what ways are you a wonderful friend, coworker, partner, or family member? I don't have many friends, to be honest, but I do have a partner whom I dote on. I always take the time to listen to her and make her feel important, no matter how busy I am. She knows she can count on me, and I'm proud of myself for gaining that trust.

Think of a time when you did something kind or generous for another person, and write about it. I once pulled over on the side of a busy highway to help a guy whose truck had broken down. I happened to have some tools in the back of my car, and I used to own a late nineties Toyota Tacoma myself, so I was able to help him get it running again. Standing in the hot sun at the side of the noisy highway for two hours was unpleasant to say the least, but I'll never forget his look of relief and gratitude when the engine started, saving him a tow truck ride he couldn't afford. I felt great for days after that happened.

Think of a time when you persevered to solve a problem, and write about it. When my mom was sick with cancer, the local hospital didn't have the right specialists to help treat it. I tracked down an oncologist three hours away who specialized in her condition, and spent hours on the phone with the insurance company convincing them to cover the visits. Even though they tried to shut me down many times, I succeeded in getting her treatments authorized. I'm not sure if my mother would have survived if I hadn't persisted.

The client who wrote these words considered himself to be pathetic and ineffective—a total loser, according to his inner judge. But when he consciously recalled his own positive attributes, and the times in his life when he'd made a difference, a different portrait began to emerge. This "total loser" had helped a stranger on the side of the highway, and succeeded at getting critical medical care for his mother. This "loser" was also a dependable partner, an accomplished violinist, and an honest, kind, and fair-minded person!

When you discover how powerful this practice can be at resetting your mindset, you may just want to do it over and over again. The more you recall your positive qualities, and positive actions you have taken, the faster your judgment wound will heal.

Healing Practice: Telling Gratitude Stories

When you are mired in judgments about yourself, the people around you, and the state of the world, you lose touch with your gratitude for life's gifts. The judgment wound keeps you in a state of constant dissatisfaction in which it is impossible to be truly happy, grateful, or at ease. Healing the judgment wound requires you to get back in touch with the things you are grateful for, and reestablishing the "attitude of gratitude" that makes life worth living.

There are countless ways to practice gratitude, many of which you have probably already heard about. Although you can simply write down a list of things you are grateful for, it is even more effective to tell a gratitude *story*—a detailed account of a time when you benefited from somebody else's kindness, generosity, or foresight. Here are some prompts to get you started:

- Write about a time a stranger was kind to you. What happened, and how did it make you feel?

- Write about a time a person in your life made you feel safe.

- Write about a time you were given unexpected relief from a problem.

- Write about a meaningful gift somebody gave you.

- Write about an action you took in the past that benefited your present self.

A client of mine was a chronic fault-finder. He couldn't receive a gift without complaining that the giver hadn't really put any thought into it, or eat a meal without pointing out at least three different ways it could have been better. He was completely out of touch with his sense of gratitude, and his mind was dominated by the real and imaginary flaws he perceived in other people and in the world at large.

It took some convincing to get him to engage in a gratitude practice. But once he got started, he gained more and more momentum, until he became one of the most grateful people I've ever met. After writing down his answers to the prompts above, he went one step further and turned his answers into gratitude letters, which he sent to the relevant people—including himself. Here is one of his letters:

Dear Naomi,

I realized I never said thank you for the time you drove all the way from Big Sur to Los Angeles to pick me up from the airport. I'd been stressing out for weeks over how I was going to make it to Big Sur with all my suitcases and my bike box, and looking into all kinds of crazy and expensive options for doing it. You were a friend of my parents and

I didn't know you very well, but when you heard through them that I was moving, you immediately reached out and offered to help.

At the time, I was so overwhelmed by the demands of finding a job and housing that I never took the time to really appreciate the magnitude of your generosity. But looking back, I'm struck by how big a deal it was. And I hope you can accept my gratitude all these years later, even if I was an ungrateful little brat back then.

Sincerely,

John

Getting in touch with gratitude helped my client enjoy his life in a way that had never been possible for him before. Not only that, but he developed better friendships and relationships as a result of his ability to feel and express gratitude.

Healing Exercise: Your Ideal Parents

Many of us inherit our judgment wounds from one or both parents, whose critical voices stick in our heads long after we move out of the family home: *Oh Marie, why can't you do anything right? Why can't you be normal? Everyone else does it this way, why do you always have to be different?* By the time we're adults, we forget that these voices came from the outside, and we come to believe that these are *our* thoughts.

In this practice, I invite you to imagine your ideal parent or set of parents. What would these parents look like? How would they talk? Which values would they pass along to you? Write down your answers in as much detail as possible. You can also close your eyes and visualize these ideal parents, imagining how they would speak to you and what they would say.

A client of mine grew up with a depressed, lonely mother who was constantly sowing the fear of failure into her children, and a distant father who responded with anger when the children asked for his attention. Her inner voices were constantly warning her about the ways that all her life decisions could turn out wrong, and suggesting that she'd better not place too many demands on her friends or partner, because they'd get angry and push her away. She wrote the following about her ideal parents:

> My ideal mother would be strong and independent. She would have lots of friends to support her through tough times, and just to have fun with. I would grow up surrounded by these strong, cool women, learning the value of friendship and community. Not only

would I be close with my mom, but I would have all these other women to turn to for advice and inspiration as well.

My ideal father would be quiet and thoughtful, more solitary than my extrovert mom. He would be kind of a Zen guy—into woodworking and gardening and playing guitar. He would model the values of patience, service, and quiet contemplation. He would never let me disparage myself for my mistakes—from a young age, he would teach me to treat myself with kindness at all times.

Until she wrote about her ideal parents, my client had never realized just how damaging her real parents' influence had been. Of course she was depressed, fearful, and filled with self-judgment—she'd been raised to believe that failure was always imminent, and that the costs of failure were devastating! She began to see that the doom and gloom mentality she so despised in herself was not, in fact, hers—it was a remnant from her childhood. Not only that, but her harsh self-criticism wasn't hers, either—it was left over from her upbringing, and she could choose to set it down.

This exercise raises self-compassion, because the gap between the parents you would have wanted and the parents you actually had is usually such a wide one. Knowing that you were raised by less-than-ideal parents, how can you continue to judge yourself? If you encountered a child who had been raised in similar conditions, would you judge that child as harshly as you judge yourself? Of course not. We heal the judgment wound by recognizing that the adults in our lives are also imperfect.

Healing Exercise: Grounding Meditation

When we are deep in the judgment wound, we tend to live in our heads, consumed by thoughts and opinions, and completely out of touch with our bodies. In other words, we become ungrounded—lost in realms of thinking, judging, and worrying. A grounding meditation can help anchor us back to reality, and allow the "head trip" produced by the judgment wound to gently dissipate. Grounding is the art of stabilizing the energy in your body by connecting yourself with the earth. When you are grounded, you feel fully present: clear, centered, strong, and focused.

To start, bring your awareness to the base of your spine or tailbone. Send an imaginary grounding cord down through your spine, anchoring you all the way to the center of the earth. You can imagine the center of the earth as a big rock or crystal and wrap your cord around it. Allow your grounding cord to be what it wants to be—tree roots, a tree trunk, a beam of light shining down from the base of your spine. You might also imagine this grounding cord as a waterfall, cascading from you down into the earth.

Allow the energy of the earth to come up through this cord, filling you up. Notice how much you can hold. Can you allow yourself to get 90 percent full with the energy of the earth?

Visualize this grounding cord for as long as it feels beneficial. When you are finished, imagine pulling the cord back into your body. Afterward, you may wish to go outside and walk barefoot on the grass, do some yoga, or otherwise deepen and prolong your connection to your body.

What does it feel like to be firmly connected to the earth and your body in this way? What sensations did you notice in your body? How have your thoughts changed?

By working with this grounding meditation on a regular basis, you will loosen the grip of your thoughts and live more in your body, which translates to living more in the present. And by living in the present, you starve the judgment wound of opportunities to cause suffering in your life.

Signs Your Judgment Wound Is Healing

As the judgment wound begins to heal, you will find yourself becoming, well, less judgmental! Instead of immediately castigating yourself or others for their imperfections, you will feel a mix of compassion and curiosity. For example, you might think, *I wonder what happened to that person to make her behave that way?* instead of, *What a piece of work!* Or you might ask yourself, *I wonder why I feel the need to rush through my tasks?* instead of, *I'm such a sloppy mess all the time!* This curiosity softens the heart and expands your capacity to feel and express love—both toward yourself and others.

I could tell that my own judgment wound was healing when I stopped feeling angry and irritated when my American patients would ask me ignorant questions about Cameroon. At the same time, I became less hard on myself when it came to the ways that *I* was ignorant.

Your judgment wound is healing if you notice any of these developments:

- A kinder, gentler inner voice

- An increase in self-forgiveness

- Greater spontaneity

- A sense of happiness and ease

- Greater self-acceptance and acceptance of others

- An increase in life satisfaction

- An increased tolerance for uncertainty and imperfection

- A quieter mind

- An appreciation for the simple pleasures in life

- A swiftness to show gratitude to others

- An increased ability to be kind and encouraging to yourself and others

- A physical unburdening, as you stop self-castigating

- A return to your ideal weight, as you stop either starving yourself or punishing yourself with overeating

Hidden Treasure: Compassion

When you heal your judgment wound, the treasure of compassion is revealed. The word *compassion* literally means "to suffer with." That is, we remove the walls that separate us from them, and we strive to understand where they're coming from. Most often, the behaviors we judge the most harshly in other people have their origins in deep wounds. Even if we never learn the details of these wounds, we can assume that they exist, and this assumption allows us to feel compassion rather than judgment when someone behaves in a way we do not like.

The same thing goes for self-compassion. When you find yourself making a mistake, or behaving in a way that you later regret, remind yourself that you, too, are suffering, and you are doing the best you can given your wounds. By practicing self-compassion, you can develop a loving relationship with yourself. This loving presence becomes a gift to everyone around you, radiating outward to touch everyone in your field. Knowing that you are not better or worse than anyone else, you can look into another person's eyes and say a sincere *namaste*—the light in me sees and acknowledges the light in you with love, grace, and presence.

Part 5

The Separation Wound

When I was eleven years old and reading Frank Herbert's famous science fiction novel *Dune* for the second time, I realized that I felt more connected to the characters in the book than to my family, my friends, or anybody I knew in my real life. This realization was accompanied by a profound sense of loneliness. For a long time, I'd felt myself to be a kind of alien. I didn't like the same things my parents liked. I didn't enjoy visiting our relatives, and I felt that, in general, social interactions were no more than a burden requiring me to put on a show and behave in a certain way, when I would have preferred to stay by myself and do what I wanted to do.

I spent all my free time reading or studying, not really being present with other people or participating in the life around me. Instead, I lived vicariously through the novels I read in my bedroom. Because I excelled at school, everyone left me alone. Instead of noticing how isolated I had become, my parents praised me for being so studious, normalizing my state of separation. I only engaged with other people when I needed something—a snack, a ride somewhere—and then I would retreat.

At the time, I was not aware of feeling lonely. The books I read were a kind of drug, capturing my attention and keeping me from feeling my own pain. The truth is, my trust had been broken so many times that I no longer saw the point in connecting with other people—deep down, I believed it would only result in me getting hurt.

This separation from others was accompanied by a separation from my own body. I lived from the neck up, safe and comfortable in the confines of my own mind. This allowed me to avoid the uncomfortable feelings of dread that lived in my gut, and the sorrow that weighed down my heart. The body is a repository of unprocessed emotional pain, and so it was only natural that I escaped into my head, using novels to dream myself into a whole new life. I rarely went out into nature, and instead stayed in my room, cut off from the sensual world.

But the worst separation of all was my separation from the divine. Like nearly 40 percent of the population in Cameroon, my family was Catholic. On Sunday mornings, my grandmother would dress my sister and me in frilly, uncomfortable dresses and take us to Mass. When I was very little, I loved going to church—it was fun to dress up, and run up and down the aisles before and after the service. I had an innate sense of connection to the divine, and could even see and feel angels at church. But as I grew into a preteen, I lost that ability. By the time I was twelve, I felt that God had abandoned me.

This feeling of being completely alone came to dominate my life for the next several decades. I felt like a kite floating aimlessly through the sky. I longed to recapture the feelings from my early childhood, that magical sense of being in touch with God, but no matter how hard I tried, I couldn't seem to conjure it back up. The despair I felt was intense. I often cried late into the night, asking myself, "How did I get so lost? How did I disappear so completely?" My body ached, and I felt like I would go mad. I truly felt that the absence of divine love could kill—that a person could literally starve to death from the lack of it. That's when I realized the most painful thing a human being can experience is separation from the divine.

Although it took me years to realize it, I was living with a separation wound. I had become disconnected from my own divinity, and from the divinity of the universe. I'd lost sight of myself as one small piece in a web of life, and instead experienced myself as a kind of island in a harsh, vast sea, with nothing attaching me to anything else. As a result of this state of separation, my batteries were constantly drained. I even woke up tired after ten hours of sleep, because my body could not replenish itself alone.

The truth is, we are all part of the divine, and we all come to this earth with special gifts, missions, things we want to learn, and things we're meant to teach to others. You might call this bundle of attributes your soul purpose, your calling, your dharma, or even your destiny. When you are tapped into these things, life feels meaningful, even when the going gets tough. You know that the people around you are likewise fulfilling their soul purpose, and that difficult people and situations are just teachers in disguise. Most importantly, you realize that you are never alone—you are always surrounded by loving and benevolent forces, both seen and unseen, who are with you even in your darkest moments.

Origins of the Separation Wound

You receive a separation wound when your relationship with the divine is severed or was never nourished in the first place. For many of us, this means growing up in a religious tradition that feels hollow, hypocritical, or false, or growing up in a consumer society in which we do not speak of the divine at all, much less feel its presence in our daily lives. Whether or not you grow up in a religious family, you may feel that the world is basically inanimate, and that the point of life is to acquire status and possessions that you must then defend from all outside threats.

This state of separation from the divine often extends to separation from other humans, from your own body, and from the earth. Instead of seeing other people as members of one human family, you may see them as hostile competitors for limited resources. Instead of seeing nature as your home, you may live a mostly indoor lifestyle, disconnected from the cycles of the soil, sky, and water. You may ignore your body, living in your head as much as possible. Finally, you may be separated from your own purpose, unable to find meaning in your life.

The separation wound can occur in several ways:

- Witnessing hypocrisy at your church or within your spiritual community

- Having an important figure in your life invalidate your sense of God or the divine

- Experiencing rejection from your community early on

- Being frightened out of your body by a traumatic experience

- Having your parents emphasize self-sufficiency and teaching you to never rely on other people

- Being raised with an "all work and no play" mentality

- Growing up without a strong community or sense of place

- Not spending a significant amount of time in nature as a child

- Being taught that nature is something to be used and abused

- Growing up with a materialistic understanding of reality

- Having parents who rarely expressed awe or wonder

- Having parents who expressed a high degree of social anxiety

In some ways, all of modern culture is suffering from a separation wound. Our culture devalues the simple pleasures of hanging out with neighbors, playing with children and animals, and soaking in natural beauty, in favor of the consumer values of acquiring big houses, expensive toys, and fancy vacations. We emphasize high-paying jobs rather than meaningful ones—and the most highly paid jobs are often the most destructive ones, while meaningful jobs often pay very little. Worst of all, we either deny the existence of the divine altogether, or we relegate it to organized religions that argue amongst themselves and frequently exclude certain categories of people. With all these things in mind, it's no wonder that so many of us are walking around with separation wounds.

I remember visiting my father's village when I was growing up in Cameroon. As a child, I found it annoying and unsettling that everyone in the village knew everyone else—and even knew all about me. When I walked around, people would say things like, "That's Marie, daughter of Essomba, who is the firstborn of Elder Essomba and lives across the river on the left side of the road." Hearing people talk like this, I felt naked and exposed. I couldn't wait to get back to the anonymity of our home in the city.

But as an adult, I smile when I recall that village. The people who lived there were truly connected.

They had deep, enduring relationships not only with each other, but with the land they lived on and with the divine, which they expressed through music and dance. The structure of tribal life formed a protective matrix around its members, making sure that nobody became too separate. Although their lives were not free of hardship, the inhabitants of that village were largely free of separation wounds—something we cannot say here in the West.

Signs You Are Living with a Separation Wound

The defining feature of the separation wound is a sense of being unplugged—from yourself, from the earth, from the human community, and from the divine. When you are unplugged in these ways, you feel exhausted, drained, and deeply alone. You may settle for a life that doesn't suit or inspire you, losing yourself to hours of TV watching or social media scrolling, or wasting away in a job or field that you've outgrown. You have little trust in yourself or others, and therefore find it difficult to take the risks that would help you grow. Because you are disconnected, you may not feel that you belong anywhere, even in a home where you have lived for years.

When I was living with a separation wound, I had no trust in life, so I felt like I had to control everything. My need for control kept me in a constant state of anxiety. I spent hours trying to predict the outcome of every decision and action I might take, striving to eliminate all uncertainty. I had zero trust that my life was unfolding in a meaningful way, and no sense that God, the universe, or anyone else had my back. Life felt harsh, lonely, and difficult.

Here are some signs you may be living with a separation wound:

- Your life is out of sync with your values, or you don't know what your values are.

- You don't feel you belong anywhere.

- There's nowhere that feels like home.

- You're not living up to your potential.

- You rarely feel a spontaneous sense of joy or gratitude.

- You avoid interacting with others beyond a superficial level.

- You find it difficult to receive gifts or favors from others.

- You are a workaholic and find it hard to do nothing.

- Your life feels mundane, pointless, and flat.

- You rarely feel at one with other people, with nature, or with the universe.

- You have a hard time asking for help, or have little trust that other people can or will help you.

- You end up in codependent relationships, because it is easier for you to feel other people's emotions than to identify your own.

- You become an over-observer, watching others instead of participating.

The separation wound keeps you in a state of exhaustion, disconnection, and victimhood. Life feels like a struggle—instead of surfing the wave, you're swimming against the current.

Here are some common ways the separation wound shows up.

Being Bored

When you are separated from your soul's purpose, life can feel flat and gray. Even if you are living in a beautiful place, with a great job and all the money you need, you might feel depressed, empty, and alone.

A client of mine was the principal engineer at a top software company in Silicon Valley. He was surrounded by some of the most intelligent people in the world, and worked on fascinating problems. His partner was an actress, and on the weekends their home was the site of spectacular dinner parties where beautiful, famous, and successful people rubbed shoulders and exchanged ideas. He was also a serious mountain biker, and traveled the world competing in—and winning!—races.

Yet for all this, my client felt listless and ill at ease. His self-image was entirely dependent on his career and his possessions. He feared that if he stopped being able to do his job—for example, as a result of a brain injury or simply from old age—his life would immediately cease to have meaning. He also struggled with a pervasive sense of boredom, like he'd already cracked the game of life and now there was nothing left to do.

As a child, my client had been taught that success was the most important thing in life. In fact, his parents hardly seemed to notice him at all unless he was waving a trophy or a perfect math score in their faces. They shuttled him from one after-school activity to another, with little downtime. He got the message that it was not OK to just play or exist— one must always be achieving something. Even as an adult, his activities were all very goal-oriented, and he felt deeply uncomfortable lying in a hammock, daydreaming, or doing other relaxing activities. He was completely separated from his innate birthright to simply be—he had become a human do-ing, and he was suffering for it.

Being Fearful

When you see yourself as separate, the world becomes a very scary place. After all, if the only person you have to rely on is yourself—and you feel small, limited, and vulnerable—you quickly learn to play it safe.

I'll never forget the time a client of mine showed up for a session in tears. That weekend, she'd driven down the coast on a mini-vacation, when she'd spotted two hitchhikers on the side of the road. They were young, sweet, and dressed in colorful clothing, and she had the uncharacteristic reflex to pull over and pick them up.

"Where are you going?" she asked them.

They said they were going to the same quaint beachside town that she was headed to herself.

"Where are you going to stay?" she asked, surprised.

"Oh, I don't know," said one of the hitchhikers. "We'll camp on the beach, or maybe we'll make friends at the drum circle tonight and they'll offer us a place to stay."

My client was amazed. She'd obsessed over the details of her own weekend at the beach—checking the traffic, pondering alternate routes, booking a hotel room weeks in advance, making sure there would be parking and Wi-Fi, even figuring out where to get coffee in the morning. She felt that she had to control every little detail—because who else was going to take care of it for her? Even though she was going on vacation to relax, she felt tense and overwhelmed.

In contrast, the hitchhikers seemed perfectly relaxed and happy. They demonstrated a trust in the universe that was completely missing from her own life.

"I don't know how else to explain it," my client told me, wiping away her tears. "It was as if they believed in God."

This encounter showed my client just how *little* faith she had in a benevolent universe, and how disconnected she had become from a felt sense of the divine. Even though she had far more material resources than the hitchhikers, she realized they were richer than her in some pretty important ways. They were connected to each other, to the divine, and to the rest of humanity, whereas she was isolated. Although she had had early flashes of this divine state of connection as a child, her parents had always taught her to not believe in "mystical bullshit" and to focus her efforts on material security.

As a result of this separation, her mind was dominated by fear. She feared not having enough; she feared not *being* enough; she feared being unprepared or vulnerable. She rarely took risks or engaged in activities whose outcomes she couldn't accurately predict. Because she was disconnected from the divine source, which is infinite, she saw life through a lens of scarcity. Until she met the hitchhikers, she rarely perceived the divinity in other people—so she refrained from making connections, receiving kindness, or asking for help.

Feeling Isolated

A client of mine grew up moving with his family from one Army base to another, with no ongoing connection to any specific place or community. The bases usually didn't have much in the way of access to nature, so kids tended to play video games indoors, or go to the mall. At a young age, he learned that there was no point in making close friends or getting involved with sports or activities, because his family would just move again in a year or two. Instead, he was aloof—socializing with other kids, but not getting truly invested; putting up a few posters in his bedroom, but otherwise not putting too much effort into making a space his own.

As an adult, he had somehow managed to recreate this pattern. He changed jobs frequently, moving from town to town just about every year. He rented cheap rooms or apartments and didn't bother furnishing them, figuring he was only going to leave anyway. Instead of putting in the effort to make real friends, he spent his evenings drinking at bars, where he could have a simulated experience of sociability aided by alcohol.

When he came to me for help, his girlfriend of five months had just broken up with him because he couldn't commit or even say "I love you." She told him she felt like a temporary piece of furniture in his life, just like his air mattress and his cheap bookshelves—designed to be left behind. Even though he *did* love her, he assumed it was his destiny to be alone—he literally didn't know how to sustain a connection for more than a few months at a time. He told me he felt like a visitor from another planet, wandering around but never truly belonging anywhere or with anyone.

Risks of the Separation Wound

Left untreated, the separation wound can cause serious misery. When you are cut off from the things that make life worth living, it's only natural to question what you're doing here on earth. This state of depression can be self-perpetuating—the more depressed you are, the harder it becomes to connect with the people, places, and practices that can restore your heart and soul.

Although living with a separation wound can be devastating, know that you can always plug back in—starting today. As humans, we are wired for connection. Although this ability may be dormant in you right now, it can be brought to life no matter how old you are or how alienated you may feel. Our brains were designed to seek out friendship, community, and mutual aid. Not only that, but we were designed to feel at home in nature, and to feel the sense of awe, wonder, and gratitude that characterizes experience of the divine. In the next chapter, I will share my favorite practices for doing exactly that.

Part 5

Healing Practices

After I became aware of my separation wound, I decided to go on a self-guided shamanic journey to learn more about the nature of my wound and where it had come from. I made myself comfortable, got out my drum, and meditated for over an hour, allowing the beat of the instrument to carry me deep into my subconscious. Over the course of this journey, I saw myself as a fetus in my mother's womb. I felt the intense hatred she bore toward my father, and heard her thoughts, which were focused on her desire to divorce him. Deep in her womb, I felt no joy or reassurance, just waves of hatred, anger, and fear. I felt unwelcome, helpless, and trapped. Although I would have liked to return to the divine, it was too late for me to go back—I had to be born to a mother who didn't really want me.

As a result of this shamanic journey, I realized that my separation wound had its origins in being disconnected from my mother's love before I was even born. For the first time, I realized that this painful separation wasn't about me; it was about her and the problems she was going through at the time I was conceived. From that point on, I began to call for the divine to come back into my life. I cried, prayed, sang, and wrote poetry. No matter where I was or what kind of work I was engaged in, I called for the divine to come meet me there.

I realized that love was all around me—I'd just cut myself off from it. I realized, too, that love was inside of me—my core, my nature, my essence, my origin, and my destiny.

In the middle of all this healing work, I was moving to a new apartment and had a strict deadline for getting all of my possessions out of my old place. The morning I was supposed to move, I was walking home from the coffee shop when I tripped on a curb and sprained my ankle. I was sitting on the sidewalk, wincing in pain, when my friend who was supposed to help me move called to say that her truck had broken down.

My mind instantly flooded with feelings of panic, anxiety, and incipient shame. What was I going to do? New tenants were supposed to move into my old apartment that very afternoon, and I'd promised the landlord I'd be out of there by noon. Even though I'd lived in Los Angeles for nearly ten years, I couldn't think of a single person I could call for help. I had dozens of coworkers at the hospital, and had lived in a building with dozens of neighbors—but I only knew these people in passing. When I thought about calling one of them, my stomach cramped with anxiety.

I felt ashamed of my own isolation. Who lives in the same city for ten years and only makes one friend? I supposed I would have to get a moving company to come last-minute, if such a thing was even possible. But when I started making calls, each company told me there was no way they could come right away. Still sitting on the sidewalk, with my ankle swelling up and my coffee getting cold, I began to cry.

A few minutes later, a woman walking her dog stopped and asked me if I was alright. "You should get some ice on that ankle," she said kindly. "My name is Alice. I live right over there. Why don't you come sit on my porch and I'll get you fixed up?"

She helped me hobble to her porch, and I petted her dog while she went inside to get the ice. Then we sat together, and I explained my predicament.

"Oh gosh," she said. "Well, my son and his friend are coming over any minute to paint my living room. If you can spare a little cash, I'm sure they'd be happy to help you move instead."

Sure enough, as we were sitting there, two twentysomethings drove up in an old pickup truck. "Josh, Esteban, this is Marie," the woman said. "She needs help moving, and I told her you might be available."

I felt a kneejerk sense of guilt and shame about accepting help—how embarrassing not to be completely self-sufficient! But before I knew it, the young men were loading my boxes into the back of their truck. They drove me to my new place and unloaded the boxes. That night, I joined Alice, Josh, and Esteban for dinner. From that point on, they became close friends, and I made many more friends through their social network. My sense of isolation went away, and I remembered a truth I had forgotten long ago: the universe is full of surprises. We can't predict everything—and often, it's better not to.

Ever since then, I've become more and more open to trusting in the divine, and to receiving the many gifts that are constantly flowing my way. I know I don't need to control everything, because in many ways life takes care of itself when I get out of the way. I can receive without guilt, because I know

I will pay it forward—I'm part of a vast, reciprocal web, and I belong.

Healing Practice: Receiving

From the time we are children, we're encouraged to share—share your toys, share your food. As we grow older, we're taught to give—give your time, donate your money, learn to be more giving. However, in Western culture, we are rarely taught how to *receive*. In fact, there can be shame associated with receiving: that's for poor people, weak people, people who can't do it for themselves. When somebody gives us a gift, we immediately start scheming about how we're going to pay it back—which is a way of *not truly receiving it.*

In order to heal the separation wound, we must get comfortable with receiving. We cannot be part of the web of life if we only give—that would violate the law of physics. Not only that, but we can't be good friends, lovers, or community members if we cannot receive.

In this healing practice, I invite you to go out and accept some kind of gift. This could mean accepting a massage from your partner, asking a neighbor for help moving a heavy piece of furniture, asking a stranger for directions, or even going to a free community meal or food bank and accepting nourishment you didn't pay for. When you have done one of these things, answer the following questions in your journal:

- What did it feel like to receive something without spending money or immediately returning the favor?

- What would it take for me to allow myself to receive on a regular basis?

- How would my life be different if I was at peace with receiving?

A client of mine was having trouble in his marriage—not because he couldn't give enough, but because he couldn't receive. When his mother died, he experienced unimaginable grief, but he wouldn't let his wife comfort him. Instead, he buried himself in work, and spent long hours at the gym. He told his wife he didn't want to burden her with his sadness, but the truth was he feared that allowing himself to be cared for would make him weak. His wife felt shut out and rejected. Her natural instincts to comfort him had nowhere to go.

I asked my client what it would be like to let his wife hold him for thirty minutes while he cried. He was horrified by the idea! "I couldn't do that to her," he said. "The last thing she needs is for her husband to turn into a puddle."

I suggested that this was the separation wound talking. If he could find the courage to receive his wife's love during this difficult time, he would find there was really nothing to fear.

He went home after our session and continued to avoid his wife. But one night, the grief was so intense that he left the gym early. His wife was on the couch watching a movie. He lay down and put his head in her lap. Within a few minutes, he began to cry. She stroked his head and comforted him, and he felt an incredible current of love flowing into his body. He realized he'd been cutting himself off from this wonderful, healing energy. It cost his wife nothing to give him this love—in fact, it felt wonderful to her too.

Healing Practice: Connecting with Nature

One of the most painful aspects of the separation wound is separation from nature. Although many of my clients have lived in their homes for years and decades, most of them do not know which watershed their tap water comes from, or the names of the trees and plants outside their own front door. They often can't remember the last time they walked barefoot, napped under a tree, or ate a wild plant or berry. They experience the outdoors as a place to move through on their way to another indoor space, not as a home in which they belong.

In this practice, I invite you to identify one natural place in your neighborhood that you can visit on a regular basis. This could be a river or lake, a scenic hilltop, or a forest or wetland. If you live in a big city, it could be a public park or even an abandoned lot where wild plants have taken over. I love to sit beside the ocean, giving my full attention to the rhythm of the waves.

Once you have identified the place, plan a special trip there. When you arrive, introduce yourself. You can do this silently or out loud. For example, you might say something like, "Hello, Pacific Ocean. My name is Marie. I live nearby. I'd like to get to know you, and the plants, animals, and nature spirits that live here. In return, I can offer you my care and attention."

The simple act of introducing yourself to a natural place contains surprising power. Growing up, we are often taught that nature is little more than decoration—something "out there." By introducing yourself to a place as you would to a person, you are placing yourself on equal footing with it, and therefore opening yourself to the possibility of a deeper relationship.

A client of mine was a very modern atheist tech worker who was suffering from chronic depression.

She found this exercise terribly embarrassing. "Me, talk to a *river*?" she said. Although she went jogging along the river all the time, with a podcast playing on her earphones, and would frequently sit on a park bench reading a novel over lunch, she had never really connected with the river as a living, breathing entity—something that could notice and respond to her, just as she was noticing and responding to it. In fact, the idea frightened her a little.

But with a little convincing, she agreed to leave her earphones and her novel at home and visit the river as she would visit a grandparent or other relative—with the intention of paying attention to it, and maybe even having a conversation.

At first, it felt terribly awkward to her to sit by the river with nothing to do. She quickly became bored and restless. She wanted her book or her podcast to fill the empty space. But when she finally got over her self-consciousness and introduced herself to the river, something wonderful happened.

Suddenly, her awkwardness was replaced by a sense of curiosity. She felt herself transformed from a consumer of the landscape into a participant. Her body relaxed, and her eyes and ears began to soak in details they'd ignored before. She began to receive the peace and beauty of the place (there's that word again, *receive!*) instead of feeling like she had to do something to justify her presence there.

Over subsequent visits, she developed a close friendship with the river. *You're looking so beautiful today!* she would say. Or, *River, I'm having a hard time and I don't know what to do.* Then she'd sit on its banks and watch the water flow, and sure enough the river would comfort her, just like a friend.

Without putting in too much effort, she began to recognize the plants and the birds. She got so interested in the birds, in fact, that she joined a local bird-watching group and became involved in conservation. Before she knew it, she was connected to several different communities: human, plant, animal, and aquatic. Her depression lifted as she moved from a state of separation into a state of profound interconnectedness. And it all started because she found the courage to treat a river like a friend.

Healing Practice: Lovingkindness Meditation

The separation wound can make you feel like you are all alone, disconnected from the rest of humanity. Even though you may have friends, neighbors, and family members, you might still be missing a sense that you are *part* of something—connected to a divine web that spans across space and time.

Lovingkindness meditation, or *metta*, can restore this sense of connection. This is an ancient Buddhist practice in which you first send loving energy to yourself, then to somebody you are close with, then to somebody you have a hard time with, and finally to all of humanity. There are many different variations on this practice, but here is my favorite technique:

First, sit or lie in a comfortable position.

Close your eyes, and call up a memory of a time when you were truly happy, peaceful, and at ease. Use all of your senses to summon this memory in full detail: you might visualize the memory, recall the feelings in your body, or even imagine the sounds and smells. Once you have successfully invoked these feelings of happiness, peace, and ease, let yourself soak in them like a warm bath. Stay here until you feel a strong, stable connection to these feelings.

Next, visualize a person you love. Putting your awareness into your heart, make a gentle wish for this person to experience the same feelings of happiness, peace, and ease you are feeling right now. Imagine that person smiling back at you, enjoying the wonderful feelings you are sending them.

Next, repeat the process for a person you have a hard time with. This doesn't have to be someone who has hurt you profoundly—it can merely be someone who annoys you or whom you slightly dislike.

Imagine this person happy, peaceful, and at ease. This can be a surprisingly moving and emotional experience, even if you dislike this person a great deal!

Repeat this process for as many people as you choose—people you like, people you don't like, total strangers. End your practice by wishing happiness, peace, and ease for all beings on earth.

When you practice lovingkindness, you connect to the divine love within yourself. You realize you can connect to the whole of humanity, even if you are trapped alone on a desert island. Even if you don't belong to a particular religion or spiritual community, you can always access the power of love.

A client of mine left her yoga ashram following a scandal involving one of the teachers. Although she had been an ardent follower of her guru's teachings, and had had many profound spiritual experiences while she was a student there, she now found herself questioning whether any of it was real. She yearned to reconnect with a sense of the sacred, but was wary of "running off and joining another cult," as she put it. Lovingkindness meditation gave her a safe way to cultivate profound feelings of love and connection without running the risk of having her trust betrayed by another institution or guru.

She later told me that she'd joined the ashram because of her separation wound—she wanted some authority figure to give her rules and restrictions to abide by, no matter how arbitrary or ridiculous they seemed in hindsight, because she believed that she was unworthy and needed fixing before she could give or receive spiritual love. As her separation wound began to heal, her feelings of unworthiness fell away, and she realized she could give and receive love anytime and anyplace—with no permission needed from any guru.

Signs Your Separation Wound Is Healing

I absolutely love it when my clients begin to work on their separation wounds, because the transformation I see in them from week to week is nothing short of miraculous. Caved-in chests become wide-open hearts. Weary brows give way to smiling faces. Heavy ruminations give way to happy chatter. Their eyes sparkle; their bodies seem to glow. They really do look like they've been plugged back in to some divine source of nourishment.

When I began to heal from my own separation wound, everyone who knew me commented on the change. "It's a whole new Marie!" people would say to me. But it wasn't a new Marie, not really—it was the Marie who had always been there, waiting to get plugged back in to her source. I felt like a dry seed who had finally been given water, and now I was flowering in full color for the first time.

Your separation wound is healing if you notice any of the following:

- An increase in energy, vitality, and libido
- A sense of connection to the people around you
- Newfound ease in making friends and building communities
- Less worrying about the future
- An increased ability to stay present
- Litheness and springiness in the body
- A reduction in pain
- Better sleep
- A good sense of humor
- Spontaneous feelings of joy
- Lowered inhibitions
- An increased tolerance for uncertainty
- Higher creativity
- Less stress in the face of adversity

Hidden Treasure: Surrender

When you heal the separation wound, a surprising treasure is revealed: surrender. If you've been living in a state of separation for a long time, surrender might not seem like much of a treasure at all—in fact, it might seem frightening: *Who wants to surrender? Won't something terrible happen if I let down my guard?*

Yet the ability to surrender is incredibly precious. When we surrender, we are trusting that God, the universe, and other people will take care of us. We are expressing our faith in the existence of benevolent forces—of kindness, generosity, forgiveness, and love. Think of the way that good lovers surrender to pleasure, good dancers surrender to the rhythm of the music, or even how babies and children surrender to sleep. Surrender is a blissful experience, available to those who have restored their sense of connection to a safe and loving universe. When you heal your separation wound, it's an experience that will be available to you, too.

Conclusion

The Five Teachers of the Heart

As I finished writing this book, I had a session with a client that will stick with me for the rest of my life. She had been through it all—abandonment as a child, betrayal by her former spouse, a judgmental and narcissistic mother, a distant and discouraging father, and, finally, a crushing battle with cancer that left her feeling like she was alone in the universe. Over the course of our time together, she had often wept, asking how she could ever recover from the level of wounding she had experienced.

Yet when she showed up for a session this one day, she had a new lightness around her. "What happened?" I asked her. "Marie," she said, "I heard my wounds *talking*. And I realized they're not me. They're actually teachers who have come to help me grow."

She remembered the way her high school soccer coach had made the team run laps and do endless burpees, until they were so strong and in shape that their bodies could handle any demands. "I *hated* that coach," she told me. "But when I started to commit to the burpees instead of resisting them, I really did get stronger. When I stopped distracting myself and actually listened to what the coach was saying, I learned a lot about how to be a better player."

Although she had been noodling around with the exercises I gave her, she had never really committed to them until that moment. Suddenly, she was engaging with her whole self. She started looking at her patterns with clear eyes, and identifying the ways her heart wounds were running her life. Not only that, but she was engaging with the wounds as *teachers to be learned from* instead of enemies to be eliminated.

Suddenly, her healing took on new momentum. She became conscious of the moments when she was acting from her true self versus when she was following the dictums of a wound. This simple awareness helped her to live more from her true self, and less from the narrow confines of her wounds. She realized that life was expansive, joyous, and brimming with possibility. I could practically see her heart glowing through her shirt, it was so radiant and alive.

Although the five wounds of the heart can be painful, uncomfortable, exhausting, or even devastating to live with, they are also our greatest teachers.

The heart contains all the wisdom we will ever need, as countless spiritual teachers have pointed out over millennia. Even the most painful corners of our hearts contain priceless treasures. If we learn to look, listen, and feel, we can apply this wisdom in our own lives, not only for our own benefit, but for the benefit of all of humanity. We can *all* become shamans, working for the greater good.

From our experiences of abandonment, we can learn to be protective, present, and caring for our friends, parents, and partners.

From our experiences of betrayal, we can learn to be discerning, loyal, and trustworthy.

From our experiences of denial, we can learn to live our truth.

From our experience of judgment, we can learn to greet life with curiosity and compassion.

From our experience of separation, we can learn to connect deeply with the heart of life.

As a shaman, I've observed time after time that the people with the deepest wounds often become the wisest healers. Our wounds are exacting teachers, but they are generous, too, dispensing their gifts as soon as we have earned them. In that sense, they are less like curses for us to break, and more like riddles for us to solve. The more we work with them, the wiser and more skillful we become.

Healing the five wounds of the heart is a lifelong process. Although you may make great leaps and experience tremendous benefits, there is always more work to be done. I know that I am always circling back year after year, discovering even deeper levels at which I can heal my wounds and release myself from the bonds of my past. Every time I return to a specific wound, I see things I'd never noticed before—and I get the opportunity to heal them. In that sense, heart wounds are gifts that keep on giving, always training us at the level we are ready for.

As you go forward and work and rework the practices in this book, I offer you all the love and encouragement my heart can hold. I know that this work takes courage. It draws on our deepest reserves of strength and vulnerability. But it is worth it. When you feel your heart in its full splendor—vibrant, alive, and radiant—you will know that everything you have experienced up until this moment was essential to your path, and that your wounds were only stepping stones leading you toward greater wisdom, compassion, and love.

About the Author

Dr. Marie Mbouni is a practicing M.D., energy healer, shaman, and artist. She was born and raised in Cameroon, Africa before relocating to Los Angeles in 2000. Her mission is to help others experience healing in all aspects of life.

Hier⊙**phant**publishing

books that inspire your body, mind, and spirit

San Antonio, TX
www.hierophantpublishing.com